GLOBALVIEWPOINTS

| Health Care

D1268302

DATE DUE

	PRINTED IN U.S.A.

Other Books of Related Interest:

At Issue Series

Cancer

Do Veterans Receive Adequate Health Care?

Health Care Legislation

Current Controversies Series

Alternative Therapies

The Uninsured

Introducing Issues with Opposing Viewpoints Series

Obesity

Vaccines

Opposing Viewpoints Series

Mental Illness

Nutrition

GLOBALVIEWPOINTS

▌Health Care

Noël Merino, Book Editor

GREENHAVEN PRESS
A part of Gale, Cengage Learning

GALE
CENGAGE Learning·

Detroit • New York • San Francisco • New Haven, Conn • Waterville, Maine • London

Elizabeth Des Chenes, *Managing Editor*

© 2012 Greenhaven Press, a part of Gale, Cengage Learning

Gale and Greenhaven Press are registered trademarks used herein under license.

For more information, contact:
Greenhaven Press
27500 Drake Rd.
Farmington Hills, MI 48331-3535
Or you can visit our Internet site at gale.cengage.com

Articles in Greenhaven Press anthologies are often edited for length to meet page require-ments. In addition, original titles of these works are changed to clearly present the main thesis and to explicitly indicate the author's opinion. Every effort is made to ensure that Greenhaven Press accurately reflects the original intent of the authors. Every effort has been made to trace the owners of copyrighted material.

Cover image © Reynold Mainse/Design Pics/Corbis.

LIBRARY OF CONGRESS CATALOGING-IN-PUBLICATION DATA

Health care / Noël Merino, book editor.
    p. cm. -- (Global viewpoints)
    Includes bibliographical references and index.
    ISBN 978-0-7377-5654-8 (hardcover) -- ISBN 978-0-7377-5655-5 (pbk.)
    1. Medical care. 2. Health services accessibility. 3. Communicable diseases--Prevention. 4. Human rights. I. Merino, Noël.
    RA411.H415 2012
    362.1--dc23
                                                                    2011048764

Printed in the United States of America
  2 3 4 5 6   16 15 14 13 12

FD184

Contents

Chapter 1: Access to Health Care Around the Globe

The Chinese government has a plan to improve access to health care for the millions of citizens who lack health insurance.

Chapter 2: The Quality of Health Care

Chapter 3: The Cost of Health Care

Taiwan's single-payer national health insurance system provides affordable health care that is superior in many ways to other advanced nations.

Chapter 4: Disease-Related Challenges for Health Care

Vaccination efforts in India have almost completely eliminated polio, but vaccination and close surveillance need to continue for the efforts to be successful.

Foreword

"The problems of all of humanity can only be solved by all of humanity."
—*Swiss author Friedrich Dürrenmatt*

Global interdependence has become an undeniable reality. Mass media and technology have increased worldwide access to information and created a society of global citizens. Understanding and navigating this global community is a challenge, requiring a high degree of information literacy and a new level of learning sophistication.

Building on the success of its flagship series, Opposing Viewpoints, Greenhaven Press has created the Global Viewpoints series to examine a broad range of current, often controversial topics of worldwide importance from a variety of international perspectives. Providing students and other readers with the information they need to explore global connections and think critically about worldwide implications, each Global Viewpoints volume offers a panoramic view of a topic of widespread significance.

Drugs, famine, immigration—a broad, international treatment is essential to do justice to social, environmental, health, and political issues such as these. Junior high, high school, and early college students, as well as general readers, can all use Global Viewpoints anthologies to discern the complexities relating to each issue. Readers will be able to examine unique national perspectives while, at the same time, appreciating the interconnectedness that global priorities bring to all nations and cultures.

Material in each volume is selected from a diverse range of sources, including journals, magazines, newspapers, nonfiction books, speeches, government documents, pamphlets, organization newsletters, and position papers. Global Viewpoints is truly global, with material drawn primarily from international sources available in English and secondarily from US sources with extensive international coverage.

Features of each volume in the Global Viewpoints series include:

- An **annotated table of contents** that provides a brief summary of each essay in the volume, including the name of the country or area covered in the essay.

- An **introduction** specific to the volume topic.

- A **world map** to help readers locate the countries or areas covered in the essays.

- For each viewpoint, an **introduction** that contains notes about the author and source of the viewpoint explains why material from the specific country is being presented, summarizes the main points of the viewpoint, and offers three **guided reading questions** to aid in understanding and comprehension.

- **For further discussion** questions that promote critical thinking by asking the reader to compare and contrast aspects of the viewpoints or draw conclusions about perspectives and arguments.

- A worldwide list of **organizations to contact** for readers seeking additional information.

- A **periodical bibliography** for each chapter and a **bibliography of books** on the volume topic to aid in further research.

- A comprehensive **subject index** to offer access to people, places, events, and subjects cited in the text, with the countries covered in the viewpoints highlighted.

Global Viewpoints is designed for a broad spectrum of readers who want to learn more about current events, history, political science, government, international relations, economics, environmental science, world cultures, and sociology—students doing research for class assignments or debates, teachers and faculty seeking to supplement course materials, and others wanting to understand current issues better. By presenting how people in various countries perceive the root causes, current consequences, and proposed solutions to worldwide challenges, Global Viewpoints volumes offer readers opportunities to enhance their global awareness and their knowledge of cultures worldwide.

Introduction

"Countries vary dramatically in the degree of central control, regulation, and cost sharing they impose, and in the role of private insurance."

—Michael D. Tanner,
*"The Grass Is Not Always Greener:
A Look at Health Care Systems
Around the World,"* Cato Institute,
Policy Analysis, *March 18, 2008*

Health care varies widely around the world in terms of access, quality, cost, and disease-related challenges. Nonetheless, many of the health care issues faced by different countries are similar in nature: How can access to health care be enhanced? How can the quality of health care be improved? What can be done to control rising health care costs? What challenges exist in fighting disease, and how should they be addressed? All over the world, individual countries and international organizations have approached these issues in diverse ways, yielding varied results. Debate abounds about the best way to improve health care and about how the health care systems of individual countries compare.

One of the perennial challenges surrounding health care around the globe is government involvement in ensuring access to health care. On one end of the debate are those who believe the government should take complete responsibility for providing health care for all. On the other end are those who believe government should stay out of the business of health care as much as possible, allowing the private market to provide for the health care needs of individuals. In between these two views are the bulk of the variety of positions on the role of government in ensuring access to health care.

At the extreme end of government involvement in providing health care is the single-payer health care system, where health care is delivered by a government-run system. Under a single-payer system, the government collects taxes from its citizens and uses the money to pay for health care. In the United Kingdom (UK), the government uses the taxes collected to fund its National Health Service to pay for the hospitals, doctors, and nurses who work for the government within its health care system. All residents of the United Kingdom have access to health care through the system, and there are no direct charges to the patients for medical care, except for small co-payments for prescription drugs. With the UK health care system, government takes charge both of collecting the revenue for health care services and of providing the medical care.

Other single-payer health care systems in the world collect taxes to finance health care but allow health care to be delivered by the private sector or by a mix of public and private health care providers. In Taiwan, for example, the government provides a mandatory insurance plan and disperses payment for health care. Health care providers, however, are private— not employed by the government as in the United Kingdom— although the government does regulate the fees that may be charged to patients in order to get reimbursed.

An alternative to the single-payer health care system that still provides universal coverage can be found in Germany. In Germany, the health care system is funded by both public and private funds. Health insurance is mandatory in Germany; although most Germans have public health insurance, they are permitted to purchase private health insurance if their incomes are high enough. Public health insurance is paid for through a payroll tax split by employee and employer. The size of the public program allows government to have strong influence on the fees charged to patients, and Germans pay only small co-payments for health care.

There are countries where government does not directly provide health care access. Like Germany, Switzerland mandates that all citizens have health insurance, but in Switzerland the health insurance providers are private, encompassing both for-profit companies and nonprofit entities. Employers do not pay for health insurance in Switzerland; each individual must pay the entire cost of his or her insurance, although there are many types of insurance from which to choose. In the case of individuals who cannot afford insurance premiums, the government offers a subsidy to purchase insurance but does not provide any insurance directly. As far as health care delivery, there are private and public hospitals in Switzerland. Swiss insurance companies work to set fee schedules for health care, with government oversight, and the Swiss pay co-payments according to the insurance plan purchased.

Other countries, such as South Africa and the United States, have a mix of both public and private health care. In South Africa, the wealthy population largely uses the private system, whereas the poor use the public system. Similarly, in the United States, the Medicaid public health care program serves low-income people, the Medicare public health care program serves senior citizens, and the rest of the population either has private health insurance or is uninsured.

According to a 2008 poll of twenty-one nations by the Program on International Policy Attitudes, through its World PublicOpinion.org project, on average 92 percent of people in various nations believe that government should be responsible for ensuring that its citizens can meet the basic need for health care. Of the countries polled, only in Egypt, India, the Palestinian territories, Thailand, and the United States did less than 90 percent of people believe that government should be responsible for ensuring that people can meet their basic health care needs. The United States had the highest percentage among any nation polled—21 percent—of people who affirmatively said that government was not responsible.

Even with the majority of people around the world assenting to the view that government should guarantee access to basic health care, as the examples mentioned demonstrate, there are several different ways for government to guarantee access. The many different health care systems in the world, along with the issues of access, quality, cost, and disease-related challenges, are explored in *Global Viewpoints: Health Care.*

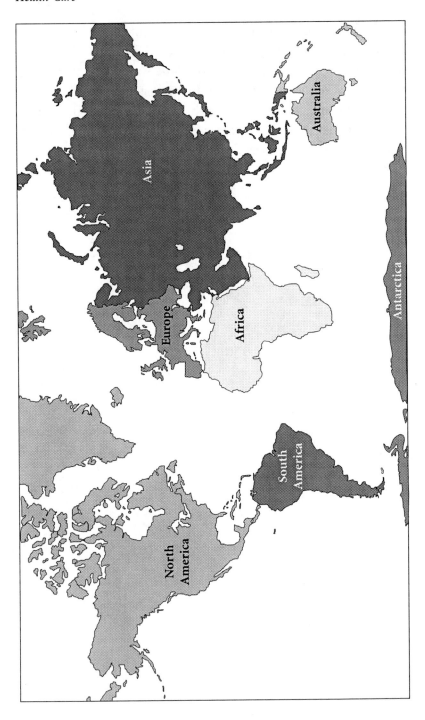

Access to Health Care Around the Globe

In Developed Countries, Most People Have Access to Health Care

Organisation for Economic Co-operation and Development (OECD)

In the following viewpoint, the Organisation for Economic Co-operation and Development (OECD) uses data from its high-income, developed member countries to assess health care. The OECD contends that the vast majority of its member countries provide universal coverage for basic health care for their citizens. Nonetheless, the OECD does claim that in certain countries there are significant minority populations that have unmet health care needs, especially among lower-income populations. In addition, out-of-pocket spending varies across OECD countries, with a small number of households facing exorbitant health care expenditures each year. The OECD is a membership organization consisting of thirty-four advanced and emerging countries dedicated to global development.

As you read, consider the following questions:

1. According to the author, what is the most common reason for unmet medical care in almost all OECD countries?

2. Which three OECD countries do not have universal health coverage, according to the author?

Michael de Looper, "Access to Care," *Health at a Glance 2009: OECD Indicators*, OECD Publishing, 2009, pp. 142, 144, 146. Copyright © 2009 by OECD. All rights reserved. Reproduced by permission. http://dx.doi.org/10.1787/health_glance-2009-en.

3. What percentage of total household consumption does out-of-pocket health spending represent in the United States, according to the author?

Most OECD [Organisation for Economic Co-operation and Development] countries aim to provide equal access to health care for people in equal need. One method of gauging equity of access to services is through assessing reports of unmet needs for health care for some reason. The problems that patients report in getting care when they are ill or injured often reflect significant barriers to care.

Unmet Health Care Needs

Some common reasons that people give for unmet care include excessive treatment costs, long waiting times in order to receive care, not being able to take time off work or caring for children or others, or that they had to travel too far to receive care. The different levels of self-reported unmet care needs *across* countries could be due to differences in survey questions, sociocultural reasons, and also because of reactions to current national health care debates. However, these factors should play a lesser role in explaining any differences in unmet care needs among different population groups *within* each country. It is also important to look at indicators of self-reported unmet care needs in conjunction with other indicators of potential barriers to access, such as the extent of health insurance coverage and out-of-pocket payments.

In most OECD countries, a majority of the population reports no unmet care needs. However, in a European survey undertaken in 2007, a significant proportion of the population in some countries reported having unmet needs for medical care during the previous year. Generally, more women than men reported not getting the care they needed, as did people in low-income groups.

Three possible reasons that might lead to access problems are presented. . . . In almost all countries, the most common reason given for unmet medical care is treatment cost. This was especially so in Portugal, Poland, Italy and Greece, and persons in the lowest income quintile were most affected. Waiting times were an issue for respondents in Italy, Poland, Sweden and the United Kingdom [UK], and affected both higher and lower income persons. Travelling distance did not feature as a major problem, except in Norway, where one-third of those indicating that they had an unmet care need said that it was because of the distance they had to travel to receive care.

In most OECD countries, a majority of the population reports no unmet care needs.

A larger proportion of the population reports unmet needs for dental care than for medical care. Poland (7.5%), Italy (6.7%) and Iceland (6.5%) reported the highest rates in 2007. Large inequalities in unmet dental care needs were evident between high- and low-income groups in Iceland, Greece, Portugal and Denmark, as well as in Belgium, although in the latter country, average levels of unmet dental care were low.

Inequalities in self-reported unmet medical and dental care needs are also evident in non-European countries, based on the results of another multicountry survey. Again, foregone care due to costs is more prevalent among lower income groups for a number of different treatments. There are large differences in the size of these inequalities across countries, as shown by much lower levels in the Netherlands and United Kingdom than in the United States. In the United States, more than half the adult population with below-average incomes reported having some type of unmet care need due to cost in 2007. Those adults with below-average incomes who have health insurance report significantly less access problems due to cost than do their uninsured counterparts.

Universal Health Care Coverage

Health care coverage promotes access to medical goods and services, providing financial security against unexpected or serious illness, as well as improved accessibility to treatments and services. Total population coverage (both public and private) is, however, an imperfect indicator of accessibility, since this depends on the services included and on the degree of cost sharing applied to those services.

By 2007, most OECD countries had achieved universal or near universal coverage of health care costs for a "core" set of services. Generally, services such as dental care and pharmaceutical drugs are partially covered, but there are a number of countries where these services must be purchased separately.

Three OECD countries do not have universal health coverage. In Mexico, only half of the population was covered by public health insurance in 2002. The "Seguro Popular" voluntary health insurance scheme was introduced in 2004 to provide coverage for the poor and uninsured, and has grown rapidly, so that by 2007 over 80% of the population was covered. The Mexican government aims to achieve universal coverage by 2011. Public coverage in Turkey was available for only two-thirds of the population in 2003, although recent legislation has introduced universal coverage.

By 2007, most OECD countries had achieved universal or near universal coverage of health care costs for a "core" set of services.

In the United States, coverage is provided mainly through private health insurance, and 58% of the total population had this in 2007. Publically financed coverage insured 27% of the total population (the elderly, people with low income or with disabilities), leaving 15% of the population (45 million people under 65 years of age) without health coverage. Of these, more than one-half cite the cost of premiums as the reason for their lack of coverage. Recent rises in the proportion of uninsured persons have been attributed to employers, particularly smaller ones, being less likely to offer coverage to workers, and to the increasing cost of premiums. The problem of persistent uninsurance is seen as a major barrier to receiving health care, and more broadly, to reducing health inequalities among population groups.

Additional Health Care Coverage

Basic primary health coverage, whether provided through public or private insurance, generally covers a defined "basket" of benefits, in many cases with cost sharing. In some countries, additional health coverage can be purchased through private insurance. Among 26 OECD countries, seven (the Netherlands, France, Belgium, Canada, United States, Luxembourg and Ireland) report private coverage for over half of the population in 2007. In the Netherlands, the government implemented a mandatory universal health insurance scheme in 2006, with regulated competition across private insurers, thereby eliminating the division between public and private insurance for basic population cover.

Private health insurance offers 88% of the French population *complementary* insurance to cover cost sharing in the social security system. The Netherlands has the largest *supplementary* market (92% of the population), followed by Canada (67%) whereby private insurance pays for prescription drugs and dental care that are not publicly reimbursed. Approximately one-third of the Austrian and Swiss populations also have supplementary health insurance. *Duplicate* markets providing faster private-sector access to medical services where there are waiting times in public systems are largest in Ireland (51%), Australia (44%) and New Zealand (33%). The population covered by private health insurance is positively correlated to the share of total health spending accounted for by private health insurance.

The importance of private health insurance is not linked to a country's economic development. Other factors are more likely to explain market development, including gaps in access to publicly financed services, the way private providers are financed, government interventions directed at private health insurance markets, and historical development.

Out-of-Pocket Health Care Spending

Financial protection through public or private health insurance substantially reduces the amount that people pay directly for medical care, yet in some countries the burden of out-of-pocket spending can still create barriers to health care access and use. Households that have difficulties paying medical bills may delay or forgo needed health care. On average across OECD countries, 18% of health spending is paid directly by patients.

In contrast to publicly funded care, out-of-pocket payments rely on the ability to pay. If the financing of health care becomes more dependent on out-of-pocket payments, its burden is, in theory, shifted towards those who use services more, possibly from high- to low-income earners, where health care needs are higher. In practice, many countries have exemptions and caps to out-of-pocket payments for lower income groups to protect health care access. Switzerland, for example, has a high proportion of out-of-pocket expenditure, but it has cost-sharing exemptions for large families, social-assistance beneficiaries and others. There is an annual cap on deductibles and coinsurance payments.

The burden of out-of-pocket health spending can be measured either by its share of total household income or its share of total household consumption. The average share varied considerably across OECD countries in 2007, representing less than 2% of total household consumption in countries such as the Netherlands and France, but almost 6% in Switzerland and Greece. The United States, with almost 3% of

Health Insurance Coverage for a Core Set of Services, 2007

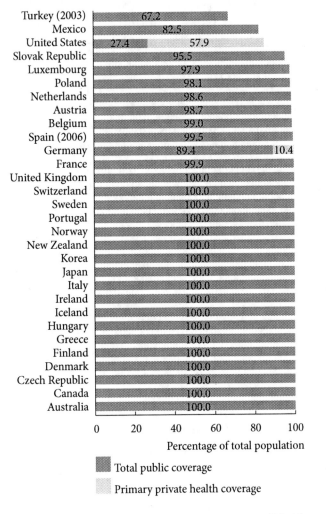

Turkey (2003)	67.2
Mexico	82.5
United States	27.4 / 57.9
Slovak Republic	95.5
Luxembourg	97.9
Poland	98.1
Netherlands	98.6
Austria	98.7
Belgium	99.0
Spain (2006)	99.5
Germany	89.4 / 10.4
France	99.9
United Kingdom	100.0
Switzerland	100.0
Sweden	100.0
Portugal	100.0
Norway	100.0
New Zealand	100.0
Korea	100.0
Japan	100.0
Italy	100.0
Ireland	100.0
Iceland	100.0
Hungary	100.0
Greece	100.0
Finland	100.0
Denmark	100.0
Czech Republic	100.0
Canada	100.0
Australia	100.0

0   20   40   60   80   100

Percentage of total population

■ Total public coverage

▫ Primary private health coverage

Source: OECD Health Data 2009, OECD Survey of Health System Characteristics 2008–2009.

TAKEN FROM: Organisation for Economic Co-operation and Development, *Health at a Glance 2009: OECD Indicators, 2009.* www.oecd.org.

consumption being spent on out-of-pocket health services, is close to the average. In 2007, 30% of US adults paid more than USD 1,000 in out-of-pocket medical costs over the past year, while only 4% of UK adults paid similar amounts. In some central and eastern European countries, the practice of unofficial supplementary payments means that the level of out-of-pocket spending may be underestimated.

On average across OECD countries, 18% of health spending is paid directly by patients.

The distribution of spending across the population can vary markedly, although data is only available for a small number of countries. The US Medical Expenditure Panel Survey found that 28% of Americans living in a poor family (defined as a family income below the federal poverty level) were spending more than 10% of their after-tax family income for health services and health insurance premiums in 2004, compared with 10% of Americans in a high-income family. Similarly, 5% of Belgian households in the lowest income decile spent more than 10% of their gross income on out-of-pocket payments in 1997, compared to less than 1% of households in the highest decile. In 2004, households in the lowest income quartile in the Netherlands spent 3.4% of their disposable income on out-of-pocket payments; in the highest quartile this was 2%.

A small proportion of households in OECD countries face "catastrophic" health expenditures each year, perhaps as a result of severe illness or major injury. Catastrophic health expenditure is commonly defined as payments for health services exceeding 40% of household disposable income after subsistence needs are met. Countries that have a greater reliance on out-of-pocket health care expenditure tend also to have a higher proportion of households with catastrophic expenditure. In Portugal, Spain, Switzerland and the United

States, rates of catastrophic spending exceed five per 1,000 people. In Mexico, the high level of out-of-pocket spending resulted in 3.4% of households having catastrophic health expenditure in 2003; among the lowest income quintile this rose to 4.7%, and among uninsured persons it was 5.1%. In some countries, the imposition of user fees may mean that lower income households forgo health care altogether, and thus do not use enough services to incur catastrophic expenditures.

In the United States, a New Law Will Help Lessen the High Number of Uninsured

Kaiser Family Foundation

In the following viewpoint, the Kaiser Family Foundation (KFF) argues that there has been a rise in the already substantial number of people without health insurance in the United States. KFF contends that the majority of those individuals who are uninsured have jobs but do not get health insurance at work or cannot afford the premiums. KFF claims that the 2010 Patient Protection and Affordable Care Act (PPACA) will help fill some of the gaps in health insurance coverage that are harming the health and financial well-being of many Americans. KFF is a nonprofit foundation that focuses on the major health care issues facing the United States and examines the US role in global health policy.

As you read, consider the following questions:

1. According to the Kaiser Family Foundation, how many Americans were without health insurance coverage in 2009?

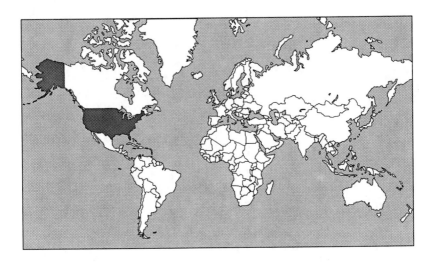

2. What fraction of the uninsured has at least one full-time worker in the family, according to the author?

3. What percentage of uninsured adults used up all or most of their savings to pay for medical bills in 2009, according to the Kaiser Family Foundation?

The deep recession and resulting decline in employer-sponsored coverage contributed to a rise in the uninsured that left 50 million [Americans] without coverage in 2009. While public insurance prevented some individuals from losing coverage, Medicaid and the Children's Health Insurance Program (CHIP) do not reach all of those who cannot afford insurance. The 2010 Patient Protection and Affordable Care Act seeks to address the gaps in our private-public insurance system. This new law will require most Americans to have health insurance and many will gain coverage through expanded Medicaid eligibility and subsidized private coverage for individuals with incomes up to 400% of poverty starting in 2014.

An Increase in the Uninsured

Recent increases in the uninsured have largely fallen on adults who have been losing employer-sponsored coverage and have been less likely to qualify for public coverage compared to children. More than one in five adults under age 65 (22%) was uninsured in 2009, which puts their health and financial security at risk.

The recent recession and ongoing weak job market has contributed to a steep rise in the uninsured. Between 2007 and 2009, the number of uninsured increased by 5 million. This trend was driven by a decline in employer-sponsored coverage, which now insures 57% of the non-elderly population, compared to 61% in 2007. The high jobless rate has helped drive the increase in the uninsured and the decline in employer-sponsored coverage. In December 2009, the unemployment rate was 10.0%—more than double the 4.6% unemployment rate in January 2007.

Workers who are offered employer-sponsored coverage have seen their costs rise. The average annual total cost of employer-sponsored family coverage reached $13,770 in 2010, and the share of the premium paid by workers increased to 30%. Since 2005, workers' contributions to premiums have gone up 47%, while overall premiums rose 27% and wages increased 18%.

More than one in five adults under age 65 (22%) was uninsured in 2009, which puts their health and financial security at risk.

Medicaid and CHIP have been crucial to preventing steeper drops in insurance coverage, and many Americans became newly eligible for these programs when their incomes declined during the recession. These programs now cover 17% of the population under age 65 and have been key to sheltering children from the full effects of the weak economy. To aid states struggling to maintain Medicaid during the recession, the American Recovery and Reinvestment Act (ARRA) provided a temporary increase in federal Medicaid funding

---

The Uninsured After PPACA

The Patient Protection and Affordable Care Act (PPACA) will expand insurance coverage by about 30 million people. Although this still falls short of universal coverage, the number of uninsured people will be reduced by more than half. Safety net providers and programs, therefore, will still face the challenge of substantial numbers of uninsured who cannot afford a full range of needed services.

Matthew Buettgens and Mark A. Hall,
"Who Will Be Uninsured After Health Insurance Reform?,"
Robert Wood Johnson Foundation, March 2011.

---

through December 2010. In the face of continuing high unemployment, Congress later extended that additional funding at a lower rate through June 2011.

The Uninsured

The majority of the uninsured are in working families. About six in ten of the uninsured have at least one full-time worker in their family and 16% have only part-time workers. About 80% of the uninsured are U.S. citizens. Uninsured non-citizens include legal permanent residents with green cards, refugees and undocumented immigrants.

Uninsured workers are more likely to have low-wage or blue-collar jobs and to work for small firms or in service industries. More than half (61%) of uninsured adults have no education beyond high school, making it difficult for them to get jobs that are more likely to provide benefits.

Those with low incomes make up a disproportionately large share of the uninsured. Some 40% of the uninsured have family incomes below the federal poverty level ($22,050 a year for a family of four). Nine in ten of the uninsured have family incomes below 400% of poverty and therefore would receive Medicaid or subsidized coverage under the new health reform law.

Aside from the elderly, who are almost all covered by Medicare, the uninsured span all ages. Young adults have the highest uninsured rate, but under the new health reform law they will now be able to remain on a parent's private health insurance plan until age 26. Children have the lowest uninsured rate, and better outreach and enrollment policies would help reach the majority of uninsured children who are eligible for public coverage.

Obtaining coverage through an employer is the most common way Americans gain health insurance. However, not all workers have access to employer-sponsored coverage. Low-income workers—those at greatest risk of being uninsured—are less likely to be offered job-based coverage and are less able to afford their share of the premiums. The new health reform law will provide additional employer incentives to provide coverage.

Those with low incomes make up a disproportionately large share of the uninsured.

Medicaid covers many low-income children, but coverage for adults is currently more limited. Parent income eligibility levels are set much lower than those of children, who may also qualify for CHIP. Unless severely disabled, even the poorest childless adults are now generally ineligible. The new health reform law will set a uniform floor for Medicaid eligibility that will extend the program to almost all individuals with incomes at or below 138% of poverty (taking into account a 5% income disregard).

The likelihood of being uninsured varies by state because of differences in employment, average incomes, and public insurance programs' eligibility levels. Uninsured rates vary more than fourfold across states (ranging from 6% in Massachusetts to 28% in Texas), with states in the South and West having some of the highest uninsured rates.

The Importance of Health Insurance

Health insurance affects access to health care as well as a person's financial well-being. Over half of uninsured adults have no regular source of health care. Worried about high medical bills, they are more than twice as likely to delay or forgo needed care as the insured. The safety net of community clinics and public hospitals is unable to fully substitute for the access to care that insurance provides.

Delaying or forgoing needed care can lead to serious health problems, making the uninsured more likely to be hospitalized for avoidable conditions. Overall, the uninsured are also less likely to receive preventive care, and consequently uninsured cancer patients are diagnosed later and die earlier compared to those with insurance.

Health insurance affects access to health care as well as a person's financial well-being.

Cost barriers to health care have been growing in the past decade, even among insured adults. But the uninsured have lost the most ground, and it impacts their health and leaves them vulnerable to high medical bills. The uninsured are three times more likely than the insured to be unable to pay for basic necessities because of their medical bills. Medical bills forced 27% of uninsured adults to use up all or most of their savings in 2009.

The weak job market has contributed to millions of Americans losing their health insurance. Additionally, rising premiums for employer-sponsored coverage and current limits on eligibility for public coverage have also left many Americans without access to affordable coverage. The new health reform law addresses these barriers to coverage through both expanded access to Medicaid and subsidies for private insurance.

The majority of the coverage expansions in the new health reform law will take effect in 2014, at which point there will be a requirement that individuals have health insurance coverage. Starting in 2014, Medicaid eligibility will be extended to virtually all of the lowest income non-elderly individuals and those with incomes up to 400% of poverty may qualify to purchase federally subsidized private coverage through a health insurance exchange. The law will also prevent insurers from rejecting individuals or charging higher premiums based on health status. The new law will decrease the number of uninsured by an estimated 32 million by 2019, leaving far fewer individuals facing the health and financial risks that come with being uninsured.

In Canada, Wait Times for Health Care Are Unacceptably Long

Bacchus Barua and Mark Rovere

In the following viewpoint, Bacchus Barua and Mark Rovere argue that the wait times to receive elective (as opposed to emergency) treatment in Canada are unreasonable. Barua and Rovere claim that long wait times are detrimental to the health of patients and bad for the economy. They argue that Canada's wait times compare unfavorably to those of other countries and note that many Canadians actually have gone abroad to receive more timely treatment. Barua is an economist at the Fraser Institute, and Rovere is associate director of the Health Policy Research Centre at the Fraser Institute.

As you read, consider the following questions:

1. According to Barua and Rovere, what was the median waiting time between referral and elective treatment in Canada in 2010?

2. How many weeks of waiting do Canadians face for ultrasounds, according to the authors?

3. According to Barua and Rovere, what two countries spend more than Canada on health spending as a percentage of their gross domestic product (GDP)?

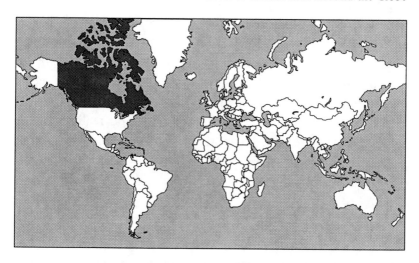

Despite the growing awareness of provincial wait times in Canada, new research shows that the issue has yet to be addressed, as Canadians are still waiting too long for access to health care.

Wait Times for Treatment

The most recent waiting list survey conducted by the Fraser Institute finds that the median waiting time between referral from a general practitioner to the receipt of elective treatment across the provinces is 18.2 weeks in 2010, up from 16.1 weeks in 2009. In order to put things into perspective, the median waiting time in 1993 was 9.3 weeks.

A peculiarity of the strategy employed by provincial governments to tackle this problem is the apparent lack of attention to the wait times patients face between the time they receive referrals from a general practitioner and when they have their first consultation with a specialist. In fact, most provincial websites do not even report this number. Given that this is an estimated 8.9-week wait, such an oversight is inexplicable. Even physicians feel that wait times in Canada often exceed what they consider to be clinically reasonable. While the study finds that physicians believe a 6.4-week wait is reasonable for elective treatment after an appointment with a specialist, Canadians actually wait for 9.3 weeks. The survey shows that, averaged across specialties, only 9% of patients are on waiting lists because they specifically requested a delay or postponement of their treatment. To clarify further the disparity that exists between the expectations and realities of the system, physicians also contend that on average, 49% of their patients would have their surgeries within a week if an operating room were available.

Wait times in Canada are longer than what is being reported in other countries.

These waiting times are undesirable for patients specifically, and for the economy more generally. Economists Ernie Stokes and Robin Somerville found that the cumulative total of lost economic output in Canada (representing the cost of waiting for treatment for joint replacement surgery, cataract surgery, coronary artery bypass graft surgery, and magnetic resonance imaging [MRI] scans collectively) in 2007 was an estimated $14.8 billion. More recently, Nadeem Esmail used average weekly wages to estimate that the cost of waiting per patient in Canada to be approximately $859 in 2009 if only hours during the normal working week were considered "lost," and as much as $2,628 if all hours of the week (minus 8 hours per night sleeping) were considered lost. Clearly, then, in addition to patient suffering, wait times also come with a significant economic cost.

A Comparison with Other Countries

One of the primary reasons (though there are many) for such long waits for treatment might be attributed to access (or lack thereof) to medical technology—something which is in dire need of attention. Canadians face a reported 4.2-week wait for computed tomography (CT) scans, a 9.8-week wait for MRI scans, and a 4.5-week wait for ultrasounds. While it is rational to have a waiting list system that places urgent cases ahead of elective ones, patients should not have to wait an inordinately long time to access the technology that is used to diagnose the severity of their condition in the first place. The Organisation for Economic Co-operation and Development (OECD) data indicate that, relative to the majority of developed countries, Canada scores poorly in terms of the availability of medical technologies. For instance, in 2007, Canada ranked 17th for both the number of CT scanners per million population (out of 26 countries), and for the number of MRI units per million population (out of 25 countries). It should come as no surprise then that wait times in Canada are longer than what is being reported in other countries.

In fact, an international comparison, conducted by the Commonwealth Fund, using survey data from 2007–2009, indicates that wait times are longer in Canada than in many developed countries. Compared to Australia, Germany, New Zealand, the Netherlands, the United Kingdom, and the United States, "Canada ranks last, or next to last on almost all measures of timeliness of care." At the same time, only two of the countries compared (the US and Germany) spent more than Canada on health spending as a percentage of their GDP [gross domestic product] in 2007.

It is clear that no matter how one looks at it . . . wait times in Canada remain unacceptably long.

One of the often-noted "qualities" of the Canadian health care system is its apparent emphasis on "equality": The notion that all Canadians, regardless of their ability to pay, must *wait their turn.* However, this year's survey of specialists found that an estimated 1.0% of patients (44,680 Canadians) received treatment in another country during 2009/10—an indication

Wait Times by Specialty, 2010

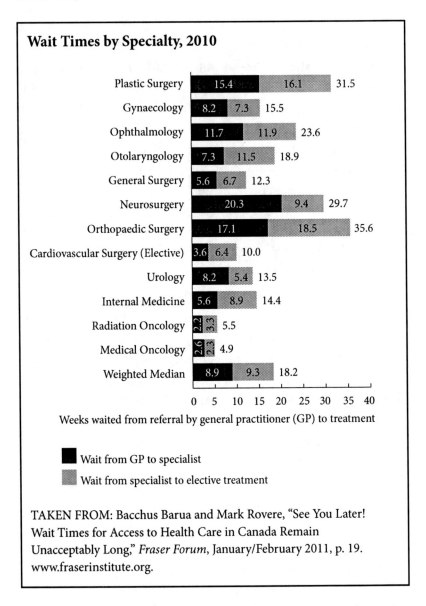

Weeks waited from referral by general practitioner (GP) to treatment

■ Wait from GP to specialist

▨ Wait from specialist to elective treatment

TAKEN FROM: Bacchus Barua and Mark Rovere, "See You Later! Wait Times for Access to Health Care in Canada Remain Unacceptably Long," *Fraser Forum*, January/February 2011, p. 19. www.fraserinstitute.org.

that Canadians who can afford it, might not only be "jumping the queue," but doing so in a *different* country.

It is clear that no matter how one looks at it—from an international perspective, in comparison to what specialists consider clinically reasonable, or simply in absolute terms—wait times in Canada remain unacceptably long.

In India, There Is Vast Inequality in Access to Health Care

Y. Balarajan, S. Selvaraj, and S.V. Subramanian

In the following viewpoint, Y. Balarajan, S. Selvaraj, and S.V. Subramanian argue that there are inequities in health in India due to inequalities in access to health care. The authors contend that there are economic and geographic barriers to accessing health care in India that affect the rural poor the greatest. Furthermore, the authors claim that out-of-pocket spending on health care is a great burden for the poor, limiting their access to care. Balarajan is a physician and a doctoral student in the Department of Global Health and Population at Harvard University's School of Public Health; Selvaraj is a health economist at the Public Health Foundation of India; and Subramanian is professor of population health and geography at Harvard University's School of Public Health.

As you read, consider the following questions:

1. According to Balarajan, Selvaraj, and Subramanian, how many years' difference is there in life expectancy between the Indian states of Madhya Pradesh and Kerala?

Y. Balarajan, S. Selvaraj, and S.V. Subramanian, "India: Towards Universal Health Coverage: Health Care and Equity in India," *Lancet*, vol. 377, February 5, 2011, pp. 505–515. Reproduced with permission from Elsevier.

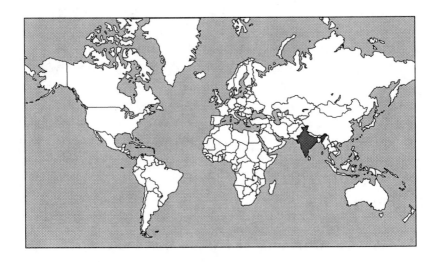

2. According to the authors, how many times more likely were Indian women in the richest quintile to give birth in an institution than were women in the poorest quintile?

3. What percentage of the Indian population is covered by some form of social or voluntary health insurance, according to the authors?

India accounts for a substantial proportion of the global burden of disease, with 18% of deaths and 20% of disability-adjusted life years (DALYs). Although the burden of chronic disease accounts for 53% of deaths (44% of DALYs), 36% of deaths (42% of DALYs) are attributable to communicable diseases, maternal and perinatal disorders, and nutritional deficiencies, which suggests a protracted epidemiological transition. A fifth of maternal deaths and a quarter of child deaths in the world occur in India. Life expectancy at birth is 63 years for boys and 66 years for girls, and the mortality rate for children younger than 5 years is 69 per 1000 live births in India—higher than the average for Southeast Asia (63 per 1000 live births).

Inequities in Health

These data, however, mask the substantial variation in health within India. Although health outcomes have improved with time, they continue to be strongly determined by factors such as gender, caste, wealth, education, and geography. Caste in India represents a social stratification: categories routinely used for population-based monitoring are scheduled caste, scheduled tribe, other backward class, and other caste; scheduled tribes (8%) and scheduled castes (16%) are thought to be the most socially disadvantaged groups in India. For example, the infant mortality rate was 82 per 1000 live births in the poorest wealth quintile and 34 per 1000 live births in the richest wealth quintile in 2005–06. The mortality rate in children younger than 5 years who are born to mothers with no education compared with those with more than 5 years of education was 106 per 1000 live births and 49 per 1000 live births, respectively, during 1995–96 to 2005–06. The variation in mortality in children younger than 5 years in different states tends to be largely associated with the extent of the economic development of the state. India has substantial geographical inequalities in health outcomes—e.g., life expectancy is 56 years in Madhya Pradesh and 74 years in Kerala; this difference of 18 years is higher than the provincial differences in life expectancy in China, or the interstate differences in the USA.

Many of the inequities in health result from a wide range of social, economic, and political circumstances or factors that differentially affect the distribution of health within a population. Since some of these inequities in health result from the unfair distribution of the primary social goods, power, and resources, the social determinants of health need to be addressed. A primary goal of public policies should be to address any inequities in health, with health systems having a special and specific role in the achievement of equity in health care and health, alongside efficiency. . . .

Inequalities in Health Care

In India, individuals with the greatest need for health care have the greatest difficulty in accessing health services and are least likely to have their health needs met. We conceptualise access as the ability to receive a specific number of services, of specified quality, subject to a specified constraint of inconvenience and cost, with use of selected health services as a proxy for access. To show the persisting inequities in health care in India, we focus on access to maternal and child health services since the disease burden relating to communicable, maternal, and perinatal disorders can be partly addressed by access to these services.

Although health outcomes have improved with time, they continue to be strongly determined by factors such as gender, caste, wealth, education, and geography.

Use of preventive services such as antenatal care and immunizations remains suboptimum, with much variation in their use by gender, socioeconomic status, and location. In 2005–06, national immunisation coverage was 44%. Immunisation coverage varies by household wealth and education, with absolute and relative inequalities generally showing reduction with time. Inequalities exist by caste—e.g., in 2005–06, immunisation coverage among scheduled tribes and scheduled castes was 31.3% and 39.7%, respectively, compared with 53.8% among other castes, and absolute inequalities between these castes increased with time. Coverage remains higher in urban areas (58%) than in rural areas (39%), although absolute and relative urban-rural differences have decreased with time. The absolute gender gap has increased from 2.6% in 1992–93 to 3.8% in 2005–06.

Similar patterns in inequalities have been noted for antenatal care coverage. In 2005–06, 77% of Indian women received some form of antenatal care during their pregnancies in the 5 years before the survey, although only 52% had three or more visits. Overall, coverage of antenatal care has improved with time. Inequalities by wealth, education, and urban or rural residence, persist, however, even though absolute and relative inequalities have decreased with time. Differences between states are substantial in both the number of antenatal visits and the type of services provided during these visits.

Inadequate access to appropriate maternal health services remains an important determinant of maternal mortality. Although the proportion of deliveries in institutions has increased with time, only 38.7% of women in India report giving birth in a health facility for their most recent birth in 2005–06. Women in the richest quintile were six times more likely to deliver in an institution than were those in the poorest quintile. Although this relative difference in inequality has decreased with time, the absolute difference in the proportion of delivery in an institution between the poorest and richest quintiles has increased from 65% in 1992–93 to 70% in 2005–06. Among scheduled tribes, delivery in an institution was 17.1% in 1998–99 and only 17.7% in 2005–06. Rates of admission to hospital also vary by gender, wealth, and urban or rural residence. Some of this variation might be due to differences in actual and perceived need and health-seeking behaviour; indeed, evidence suggests that gender inequalities exist in untreated morbidity, and illness is probably under-reported among women.

Although poor individuals are more likely to seek care in the public sector than in the private sector, rich people use a greater share of public services and are more likely to use tertiary care and hospital-based services. Rich individuals are also more likely to be admitted to hospital than are poor people and have longer inpatient stays in hospitals in the public sector. Analysis of the 52nd round (1995–96) of the National Sample Survey of health services in the public sector showed a more equitable distribution of services for preventive care (immunisation and antenatal visits) than did most of those for curative care.

Barriers to Accessing Health Care

Efficient allocation of resources between primary, secondary, and tertiary care, and geographical regions is crucial to ensure the availability of appropriate and adequately resourced health services. In India, this challenge is compounded by low public financing with substantial variation between states. India's total expenditure on health was estimated to be 4.13% of the gross domestic product (GDP) in 2008–09, of which the public expenditure on health was estimated to be 1.10%. Private expenditures on health have remained high during the previous decade, with India having one of the highest proportions of household out-of-pocket health expenditures in the world— 71.1% in 2004–05.

Per-person expenditures disbursed by the central government to states are fairly similar, irrespective of the different capabilities and health needs of the states. Expenditures on health differ by a factor of seven between the major states— e.g., public expenditure per person in 2004–05 was estimated to be INR93 [93 Indian rupees] in Bihar compared with INR630 in Himachal Pradesh. Besides interstate variations, a greater proportion of resources is given to urban-based services and curative services, with 29.2% of public expenditures (both central and state) allocated to urban allopathic services compared with 11.8% of public expenditures allocated to rural allopathic services in 2004–05. This imbalance in allocation is worsened by a bias in the private sector towards curative services, which tend to be provided in wealthy urban areas. The curative services are mainly provided in the private sector, and evidence from national household surveys shows that the private sector in the previous two decades has become the main provider of inpatient care.

Physical access is a major barrier to preventive and curative health services for India's (>70%) rural population. The number of beds in government hospitals in urban areas is more than twice that in rural areas, and the rapid development of the private sector in urban areas has resulted in an unplanned and unequal geographical distribution of services. Although the concentration of facilities in urban areas might encourage economies of scale, the distribution of services is an important factor that affects equity in health care, mainly because many vulnerable groups tend to be clustered in areas where services are scarce. In 2008, an estimated 11,289 government hospitals had 494,510 beds, with regional variation ranging from 533 people per bed in a government hospital in Arunachal Pradesh to 5494 in Jharkhand.

Since distance to facilities is a key determinant for access, outreach programmes or good transport, roads, and communication networks are important to reach disadvantaged and physically isolated groups, such as the scheduled tribes. Distance remains a greater barrier for women than for men. Furthermore, physical access of services does not assure their use since the costs associated with seeking care also preclude uptake, even when services are available.

Factors Affecting Demand for Health Care

Insufficient public financing, lack of a comprehensive method for risk pooling, and high out-of-pocket expenditures because of rising health costs are key factors that affect equity in health financing and financial risk protection. Evidence from surveys of national expenditures suggests that inequalities in health financing have worsened during the past two decades. Only about 10% of the Indian population is covered by any form of social or voluntary health insurance, which is mainly offered through government schemes for selected employment groups in the organised sector (e.g., state insurance scheme for employees, central government health scheme). The Insurance Regulatory and Development Authority Bill was passed in 1999, and private insurance companies account for 6.1% of health expenditures on insurance. Community-based health insurance schemes and schemes for the informal sector that encourage risk pooling provide for less than 1% of the population.

Individuals who are poor are most sensitive to the cost of health care; they are less likely than are those who are rich to seek care when they are ill, and this difference is more evident in rural than in urban areas. Moreover, people who are poor are most likely to report financial cost as the reason for foregoing care when they have an illness, and this effect has increased with time for individuals living in rural and urban areas. For example, the cost of maternal care is not affordable for the poorest households (lowest two deciles), when the average costs incurred during the year of childbirth exceeds their yearly capacity to pay.

Out-of-pocket expenditure on health, as a proportion of household expenditure, has increased with time in rural and urban areas. Expenditures on inpatient and outpatient health care are consistently higher in private facilities than in public facilities; and expenditure is greater for noncommunicable diseases than for communicable diseases. Notably, the proportion of money spent on health has increased most for the poorest households.

Only about 10% of the Indian population is covered by any form of social or voluntary health insurance.

The Cost of Health Care

The financial burden of inpatient and outpatient care is consistently greater for rural households than for urban households, with rapid increase in expenditures per admission. In 2004–05, about 14% of rural households and 12% of urban households spent more than 10% of their total consumption expenditure on health care. Treatment in hospital is also expensive, with more than a third of costs paid by borrowing money. Even for inpatient care, drug expenditures account for the largest burden of this cost. Drugs, diagnostic tests, and medical appliances account for more than half of out-of-pocket expenditures.

Evidence from several developing countries shows that out-of-pocket expenditures on health exacerbate poverty. Inadequate protection of financial risk against financial shocks that are associated with the costs of medical treatment have worsened the poverty in many households. Ill health and health expenditures are contributory factors for more than half of households that fall into poverty. In 2004–05, about 39.0 million (30.6 million in rural areas and 8.4 million in urban areas) Indian people fell into poverty every year as a result of out-of-pocket expenditures. These estimates do not take into account the effects on people already living below the poverty line who are pushed further into poverty or those groups who are forced to forego health care as a result of the costs. The absolute and relative effects of out-of-pocket expenditures on poverty have been increasing. The effect of health expenditures is greater in rural areas and in poorer states, where a greater proportion of the population lives near the poverty line, with the burden falling heavily on scheduled tribes and scheduled castes.

Inflation in health spending is another major factor that constrains access to health services and equity in financing. Between 1986–87 and 2004, the absolute expenditures per outpatient and inpatient visit in rural and urban areas increased, affecting the access to services for the poorest individuals. Although costs have increased in the public and private sectors, the increase has been much faster (>100% between 1986–87 and 2004) in the private sector. Increase in expenditures has been fastest for inpatient services in rural areas.

In China, There Is a Plan to Reduce the Millions Without Health Care

Veronica M. Valdez

In the following viewpoint, Veronica M. Valdez argues that China has undertaken a bold plan to reform its failing health care system that has left large populations uninsured and without access to health care. Valdez claims that China's move toward a market economy, along with a drop in state-supported health care funding, contributed to the current state of affairs. Valdez applauds the Chinese government's ambitious new plan to bring health care to the millions who are lacking it, but she concludes that it will be a challenge. Valdez is a special assistant to the assistant secretary of the US Navy.

As you read, consider the following questions:

1. According to Valdez, the Chinese government has announced an overhaul of its health care system intended to offer health services to all Chinese people by what year?

2. Chinese government funding of health care dropped to 20.3 percent in 2007 from what percentage in 1980, according to Valdez?

Veronica M. Valdez, "China's De-Socialized Medicine," *Foreign Policy*, June 11, 2009. www.foreignpolicy.com.

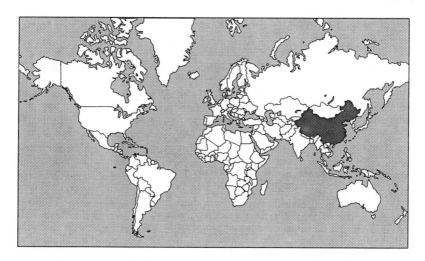

3. The author claims that as part of its overhaul, China
plans to build how many clinics, hospitals, and urban
community clinics?

The United States and China have more in common than
their paramount importance in the global economy. The
citizens of both countries share the same basic complaint: bad
health care. As the White House prepares [in 2009] to roll out
its plan to overhaul the United States' woefully inadequate
health insurance system, it may be instructive to look across
the Pacific, where an even more ambitious effort is under way
to give access to health care to the millions left behind by
China's rapid economic growth.

Today, more than 200 million Chinese lack health insurance. Soaring medical fees, lack of access to high-quality medical services, the widening rural-urban gap, and poor doctor-
patient relationships have all sparked public outcry. So after
years of incremental change, the Chinese government recently
announced a $124 billion, three-year overhaul of its health
care system that aims to provide safe, effective, convenient and
affordable health services to all of the country's 1.3 billion
people by 2020.

The government's move to spend more on health care today is critical. With a population discontented over its health care system coupled with a global economic downturn, Beijing is understandably nervous about social unrest. But while the scale of the new effort is unprecedented, the problem is hardly new.

The History of China's Uninsured

After the founding of the People's Republic in 1949, the party faced a daunting challenge. With a total population of 540 million, there were only around 40,000 physicians trained in Western medicine, the vast majority of whom lived in cities. Unfortunately 80 percent of the population lived in rural areas, and party leaders, including Mao Zedong, recognized that improving the health of farmers was crucial to increasing agricultural production and achieving the Great Leap Forward. The party launched a massive public health campaign sending out trained workers to the countryside to treat rural peasants.

Today, more than 200 million Chinese lack health insurance.

The launch of the Cultural Revolution brought health care to the forefront, with Chairman Mao making a famous health care speech in 1965 in which he declared the need to put the stress on rural areas in health and medical work. His government created a national health care policy called the cooperative medical system (CMS), a three-tiered system that included barefoot doctors, commune health centers, and county hospitals, and provided free health care to 90 percent of the population. Barefoot doctors were young peasants who received three to six months of medical training and provided free basic health care including first aid, immunizations against common diseases like measles, health education, and hygiene.

A Commitment to Health Care

While it is still too early to assess outcomes, the [Chinese] government has made it a high priority to strengthen the health care system and to do so in a way that is sustainable and avoids the fiscal problems that escalating health care costs are causing in many advanced economies. It is clear that China has a reinvigorated commitment to making high-quality health care . . . available to all China's citizens.

Steve Barnett and Nigel Chalk,
"Building a Social Safety Net," Finance & Development,
September 2010, p. 35.

Mao, of course, got many things wrong. But he got a few things right. The American Medical Association found that the CMS program reduced infant mortality from 250 to 40 deaths per 1000 births, doubled life expectancy, and drastically reduced the prevalence of infectious diseases.

As China moved toward a market-oriented economic system in the early 1980s, the central government provided less and less financial support for the CMS, transferring the cost and responsibility of health care to local governments. Urban and rural workers suddenly lost the cradle-to-grave social safety net they enjoyed during the days of the planned economy. Millions essentially became uninsured overnight.

A Broken System

China's Ministry of Health reports that government funding of health care dropped to 20.3 percent in 2007 from 36.2 percent in 1980. With local governments strapped for cash, doctors at state-run hospitals were granted permission by the central government to generate revenue by charging for medical services. This fee-for-service system continues today as many hospitals are forced to generate income to cover costs through prescribing extremely profitable (and mostly unnecessary) drugs and treatments.

As a result, the health care gap between rural and urban areas has continued to widen. In 2000, roughly two-thirds of the population lived in rural areas, but rural health expenditures accounted for only 22.5 percent of total national health spending. According to the Ministry of Health, between 1985 and 2005, the annual disposable income of citizens increased twentyfold, while the amount they spent on health care increased 133 times. Many Chinese now simply forego treatment because they can't afford it.

David Wood, a ChinaCare Group health consultant in Beijing and former senior manager at a U.S.-based hospital, told me: There is no safety net in China. . . . If you don't have money, you just don't get treatment. He cited estimates that 70 to 80 percent of health care dollars come out of patients' pockets.

The government began trying to rectify the situation in 1998 by implementing a mandated employer insurance program under which workers at private companies and state-owned enterprises had to contribute a portion of their paycheck for health insurance (totaling up to 10 percent of workers' annual wages). A program was launched in 2002 providing $2.50 a year for basic insurance for the rural population, who then contributed $1.25 of their own money to the account. Unfortunately, these programs were not as successful as hoped, and a much bigger and wider reform was needed.

A New Plan

China's new plan is far more ambitious. First, it aims to increase the percentage of the rural and urban populations covered by the basic medical insurance system or a new rural cooperative medical system to at least 90 percent by 2011. Second, the medicine supply system will be streamlined so that public hospitals and clinics are supplied with essential drugs at prices regulated by the government. Third, in the next three years, 5,000 clinics will be built in rural townships, plus 2,000 county hospitals and 2,400 urban community clinics. Additional training will be given to 1.37 million village doctors and 160,000 community doctors. Public hospital doctors will have to work for one year at rural hospitals before they are considered for promotion.

> *With health care becoming the public's top concern, Beijing has learned that privatization can negatively impact the health of citizens and that government involvement is essential.*

The new spending represents a fundamental shift in attitude on the part of Chinese leaders. With health care becoming the public's top concern, Beijing has learned that privatization can negatively impact the health of citizens and that government involvement is essential. In addition to relieving citizens' financial burden, the reform plan aims to create thousands of jobs, decrease unemployment, increase consumer spending and business investment, and reduce the incentive for the millions of rural Chinese who migrate to cities every year, overwhelming the public welfare system.

China's health reform plan is complex and will be challenging to implement. First, China will require stronger and much more stringent administrative and legal regulations than those currently in place. These reforms will also require a strict ethic of professionalism where doctors protect the interests of their patients and provide high-quality care rather than the frequent abuses that took place under the fee-for-service system.

These wide and sweeping health reforms will have profound implications for hundreds of millions of Chinese and could have a global impact as well. If the world's most populous country can get this right, it will be a monumental achievement. And health care reformers elsewhere, including the United States, may soon be looking to steal a page or two from China's book.

In South Africa, Migrants Do Not Have Adequate Access to Health Care

Human Rights Watch

In the following viewpoint, Human Rights Watch argues that South Africa is failing to meet its obligation to provide basic health care to asylum seekers, refugees, and undocumented migrants in the country. Human Rights Watch claims that South Africa's own constitution and international law require that the country provides basic care against communicable disease. Human Rights Watch claims that migrants are suffering abuses that affect their health, and the organization concludes that it is in the best interest of South Africa to protect the public health of its own country by ensuring that migrants have access to health care. Human Rights Watch is an independent, international organization dedicated to defending and protecting human rights.

As you read, consider the following questions:

1. According to Human Rights Watch, South Africa's Constitution provides for the right to health for whom?

2. South Africa has recognized what percentage of Zimbabwean asylum claims through 2007, according to the author?

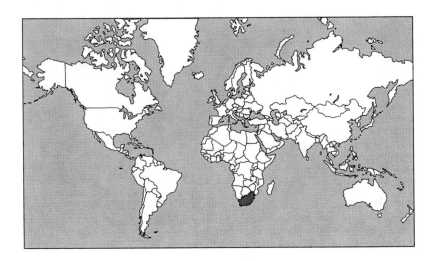

3. According to Human Rights Watch, failures to detect and treat illness and prevent injury in vulnerable populations carry what costs?

"There is no healing here in South Africa. Since I arrived here there is no rest, no recovery."

—*Ndona, Congolese refugee, Johannesburg*

Ndona speaks for the many thousands of migrants in South Africa who were made homeless by xenophobic attacks in 2008, forced to take shelter in unsafe and unsanitary camps, abandoned buildings, churches, and on open ground, where they are vulnerable to disease and further violence. Refugees like Ndona, fleeing war in places like the Democratic Republic of the Congo (DRC) and Somalia and economic and political crises in places like Zimbabwe, have found themselves without the most basic human rights fundamental to life: food, shelter, physical security, and access to basic health care. As shocking as the severity of the xenophobic violence is the fact that such widespread abuses are tolerated in South Africa, a country with some of the most expansive rights in the world for refugees and other migrants. The widespread violence and displacement leading to homelessness and unsafe living conditions, along with systemic government failures to protect migrants from arrest and deportation, has created a massive health crisis for migrants—and their hosts—in South Africa. Xenophobia, violence, and discrimination create both environments that promote risks to migrants' health as well as barriers to obtaining basic health care.

Health Care for Migrants

South Africa's Constitution provides for the right to health for "everyone" within the country. In recent years, this provision has been tested as regional crises created unprecedented numbers of asylum seekers and undocumented migrants entering there. Since 2007 the Department of Health (DOH) has repeatedly affirmed the rights of asylum seekers and refugees to access the same public health care to which citizens have access. However during this same period, documented and undocumented migrants alike have been denied access to health care. Even when seeking emergency care after xenophobic attacks or rapes, migrants are often turned away by medical personnel who may discharge them prematurely, harass them, charge them excessive user fees, and call the police to deport them.

But the risks to health and barriers to care that migrants experience in South Africa are not the responsibility of the DOH alone. The South African asylum system has failed for years to provide protection to asylum seekers and recognized refugees due to systematic problems. Restrictive immigration provisions leave many labor migrants, long an important part of South Africa's economy, undocumented and unprotected from deportation, discrimination, and ill treatment. Up to a million undocumented Zimbabweans may be eligible for asylum or for a still-unimplemented special dispensation program, but remain without protection and documentation that would facilitate their access to health care. The perpetrators of xenophobic violence have gone largely unpunished. Wherever asylum seekers, refugees, and undocumented migrants gather to find shelter in South Africa—in the remnants of closed camps, outside of government offices in cities and near the border, in abandoned garages, and in the sanctuary of churches—they are subject to health-threatening conditions, eviction, and arrest. These abuses work against the aims of the inclusive right to health professed by the South African Constitution.

Xenophobia, violence, and discrimination create both environments that promote risks to migrants' health as well as barriers to obtaining basic health care.

Meanwhile, the collapse of the public health system in Zimbabwe has created a regional health crisis that requires ongoing regional humanitarian coordination. Communicable diseases like HIV/AIDS and tuberculosis [TB] are prevalent within South Africa and throughout southern Africa, with relatively low rates of treatment success and relatively high rates of drug resistance. In one example of the inevitability of cross-border health crises, in 2008 Zimbabwe experienced a serious cholera epidemic that eventually affected South Africa, which suffered more than 12,000 infections and more than 60 deaths. Cross-border migrants, particularly those travelling informally without documents, face conditions that increase their susceptibility to infection and decrease their ability to access or adhere to treatment. Despite the risk they face, and the risks that communicable disease poses to the entire community, South Africa has largely failed to design public health initiatives that reach vulnerable mobile and migrant populations. Removing barriers to care, conducting active outreach to at-risk migrant communities, and coordinating with civil society and affected communities are necessary components of South Africa's campaign to achieve more universal access for

HIV and TB treatment. South Africa cannot achieve positive health outcomes for its own citizens while neglecting those of vulnerable migrant communities.

A Failure to Protect Migrants

Migrants to South Africa come for varied and complex reasons. . . . Asylum seekers are migrants who claim to have been forced to flee their home country because they have a well-founded fear of being persecuted on account of their "race, religion, nationality, membership of a particular social group or political opinion" as defined by the 1951 UN [United Nations] refugee convention. Those who express such a fear are protected under international law from deportation to their home countries (refoulement) pending the resolution of their asylum claims. If an asylum seeker's claim is proved to the satisfaction of the Department of Home Affairs (DHA), the asylum seeker is recognized as a refugee, a status that carries many of the same rights as permanent residency and citizenship.

Any barrier to prevention and treatment of communicable disease for vulnerable mobile and migrant populations is unwise from a public health perspective.

Any migrant who enters the country without a visa could be termed an "undocumented migrant," but in this [viewpoint] the term refers to those (largely Zimbabwean) undocumented migrants to South Africa who do not lodge asylum claims. The term is used to allow for the complex nature of recent migration from Zimbabwe, and the possibility that at least some undocumented migrants should be, or shortly will be, protected by either the asylum system or the special dispensation permit.

In its November 2005 report, "Living on the Margins: Inadequate Protection for Refugees and Asylum Seekers in Johannesburg," Human Rights Watch reported on the systemic inadequacies in the Department of Home Affairs' registration and status determination systems that have left many asylum seekers without documentation, and many legitimate asylum claims unrecognized. The asylum system has been stretched past its capacity by the sharp influx of asylum seekers from Zimbabwe fleeing political oppression, violence, economic collapse, and breakdown in public health, sanitation, and other services. Despite the extraordinary nature of the political crisis in Zimbabwe, the severity of the deprivation there and the long-documented persecution experienced by many of its émigrés, South Africa has recognized only a small minority of Zimbabwean asylum claims, approximately 20 percent through 2007. Asylum seekers from all countries continue to be left to navigate a byzantine bureaucracy to gain recognition as refugees, languishing for months and years without resolution and subject to detention and deportation as well as discrimination.

In addition to widespread violence, migrants are also especially vulnerable to communicable disease because of substandard living environments, limited sanitation, and cultural and social dislocation, making them vital targets for public health surveillance and intervention. According to Department of Health policies, everyone in South Africa should have access to treatment for communicable disease without cost. Any barrier to prevention and treatment of communicable disease for vulnerable mobile and migrant populations is unwise from a public health perspective, but also a violation of South African and international law. South Africa has recognized the importance of access to health care for vulnerable and migrant populations in its laws and policy documents yet continues to allow unlawful discrimination by health care staff, undermining efforts to contain disease and improve treatment outcomes.

Abuses Affecting Migrant Health

In over 100 interviews with migrants, advocates, health care and other service providers in both urban and border communities, Human Rights Watch found that South Africa's failure to protect asylum seekers and refugees from deportation and violence leads both to increased disease and injury, and increased barriers to treatment for those conditions.

Human Rights Watch documented two broad sets of abuses affecting migrants' health in South Africa:

• abuses leading to health vulnerability, and

• barriers to access to health care.

Human Rights Watch's researchers found asylum seekers, refugees, and undocumented migrants living in harrowing and life-threatening conditions, constantly under threat of assault, rape, disease, and discrimination. Unable to find secure accommodation, migrants were often displaced from one dangerous informal shelter to another, facing harassment and attacks by their neighbors, evictions by local governments, and police raids. Refugees and asylum seekers, even those who were documented, told Human Rights Watch that in many cases when they seek health care, clinics and hospitals either refuse to treat them, terminate their care prematurely, charge them excessive fees, or verbally harass and mistreat them for being foreign. This amounts to a failure by the South African state to protect the basic rights and safety of migrants. South Africa's failure to ensure that migrants have access to the health care services to which they are entitled compounds their medical conditions. When discrimination or other factors impede care, migrant patients tend to be diagnosed later and only treated well into the development of illness; and when they are sicker, care is more expensive and treatment tends to be less effective.

South African citizens reliant on the public health system may experience similar health vulnerabilities and access problems to those described here. Certainly, many South Africans also face resource and capacity constraints in public sector care, long wait times, abusive attitudes by staff, poor living conditions, and vulnerability to violence. However, the evidence shows that migrants, including refugees and asylum seekers, experience specific abuses in addition to the systemic failures that affect all patients, compounding the vulnerability they already face. They are actively discriminated against and they are targets of violence specifically and exclusively because they are non-nationals. Furthermore, South Africa's failures to detect and treat illness and prevent injury in vulnerable populations carry costs of their own. Illness advances, spreads, becomes resistant to first-line drugs, and becomes costlier to treat, and short- and long-term disabilities create economic dependency in migrants who would otherwise be independent and productive. For a health system that struggles to meet the needs even of its own citizens, the consequences of failing to adequately treat migrants, both to the public health and to the cohesiveness of a multiethnic South African society strained by xenophobia, cannot be ignored.

Periodical and Internet Sources Bibliography

The following articles have been selected to supplement the diverse views presented in this chapter.

Bulletin of the World Health Organization	"Flawed but Fair: Brazil's Health System Reaches Out to the Poor," vol. 86, no. 4, April 2008.
Michael P. Coleman et al.	"Cancer Survival in Five Continents: A World-wide Population-Based Study," *Lancet*, August 2008.
Elizabeth Docteur and Robert A. Berenson	"How Does the Quality of U.S. Health Care Compare Internationally?," *Timely Analysis of Immediate Health Policy Issues*, August 2009.
Rajat Gupta	"A Healthier Future for India," *McKinsey Quarterly*, January 2008.
Linda Halderman	"Healthcare Access Better Overseas?," *American Thinker*, December 12, 2009. www.american thinker.com.
Sarah Hall	"People First: African Solutions to the Health Worker Crisis," African Medical and Research Foundation (AMREF), 2007. www.amref.org.
Devon M. Herrick	"Medical Tourism: Global Competition in Health Care," *NCPA Policy Report*, November 2007.
Ross Kaminsky	"Is It a Right or Isn't It?," *American Spectator*, December 29, 2010.
Kathleen MacKenzie	"Surprised by Quality Health Care in Switzerland," *Denver Post*, March 31, 2010.
Sandhya Srinivasan	"India: Healthcare for Under $30 a Year," *World Policy Journal*, Summer 2010.

The Quality of Health Care

Health Care in the United States Is Superior in Many Categories

Scott W. Atlas

In the following viewpoint, Scott W. Atlas argues that despite the criticism the US health care system receives, there are several ways in which the American system surpasses the health care systems of other comparable countries. Atlas claims that the United States has better survival rates from disease, as well as better access to treatment and preventative care, than many developed countries. Atlas also contends that Americans are largely satisfied with their health care. Finally, Atlas claims that the United States is responsible for the majority of health care innovations in the world. Atlas is a senior fellow at the Hoover Institution as well as a professor of radiology and chief of neuroradiology at Stanford University Medical Center.

As you read, consider the following questions:

1. According to Atlas, breast cancer mortality is what percentage higher in the United Kingdom than in the United States?

2. American seniors with below-median incomes report excellent health by what factor greater than Canadian seniors, according to Atlas?

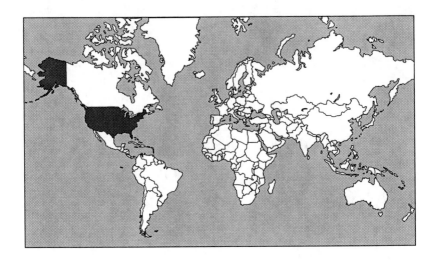

3. What percentage of Americans are very satisfied with their health care services, according to the author?

Medical care in the United States is derided as miserable compared to health care systems in the rest of the developed world. Economists, government officials, insurers and academics alike are beating the drum for a far larger government role in health care. Much of the public assumes their arguments are sound because the calls for change are so ubiquitous and the topic so complex.

However, before turning to government as the solution, some unheralded facts about America's health care system should be considered.

The Quality of U.S. Health Care

Fact No. 1: Americans have better survival rates than Europeans for common cancers. Breast cancer mortality is 52 percent higher in Germany than in the United States, and 88 percent higher in the United Kingdom [U.K.]. Prostate cancer mortality is 604 percent higher in the U.K. and 457 percent higher in Norway. The mortality rate for colorectal cancer among British men and women is about 40 percent higher.

Fact No. 2: Americans have lower cancer mortality rates than Canadians. Breast cancer mortality is 9 percent higher, prostate cancer is 184 percent higher and colon cancer mortality among men is about 10 percent higher than in the United States.

Fact No. 3: Americans have better access to treatment for chronic diseases than patients in other developed countries. Some 56 percent of Americans who could benefit are taking statins, which reduce cholesterol and protect against heart disease. By comparison, of those patients who could benefit from these drugs, only 36 percent of the Dutch, 29 percent of the Swiss, 26 percent of Germans, 23 percent of Britons and 17 percent of Italians receive them.

Americans have better access to treatment for chronic diseases than patients in other developed countries.

Fact No. 4: Americans have better access to preventive cancer screening than Canadians. Take the proportion of the appropriate-age population groups who have received recommended tests for breast, cervical, prostate and colon cancer:

- Nine of 10 middle-aged American women (89 percent) have had a mammogram, compared to less than three-fourths of Canadians (72 percent).

- Nearly all American women (96 percent) have had a pap smear, compared to less than 90 percent of Canadians.

- More than half of American men (54 percent) have had a PSA [prostate-specific antigen] test, compared to less than 1 in 6 Canadians (16 percent).

- Nearly one-third of Americans (30 percent) have had a colonoscopy, compared with less than 1 in 20 Canadians (5 percent).

Disease Survival in the United States

When you compare the outcomes for specific diseases, the United States clearly outperforms the rest of the world. Whether the disease is cancer, pneumonia, heart disease, or AIDS, the chances of a patient surviving are far higher in the United States than in other countries. For example, according to a study published in the British medical journal the *Lancet*, the United States is at the top of the charts when it comes to surviving cancer. Among men, roughly 62.9 percent of those diagnosed with cancer survive for at least five years. The news is even better for women: The five-year survival rate is 66.3 percent, or two-thirds. The countries with the next best results are Iceland for men (61.8 percent) and Sweden for women (60.3 percent). Most countries with national health care fare far worse. For example, in Italy, 59.7 percent of men and 49.8 percent of women survive five years. In Spain, just 59 percent of men and 49.5 percent of women do. And in Great Britain, a dismal 44.8 percent of men and only a slightly better 52.7 percent of women live for five years after diagnosis.

Michael D. Tanner, "The Grass Is Not Always Greener: A Look at National Health Care Systems Around the World," Cato Institute, Policy Analysis, *no. 613, March 18, 2008.*

A Comparison of Satisfaction

Fact No. 5: Lower-income Americans are in better health than comparable Canadians. Twice as many American seniors with below-median incomes self-report "excellent" health compared to Canadian seniors (11.7 percent versus 5.8 percent). Conversely, white Canadian young adults with below-median incomes are 20 percent more likely than lower-income Americans to describe their health as "fair or poor."

Fact No. 6: Americans spend less time waiting for care than patients in Canada and the U.K. Canadian and British patients wait about twice as long—sometimes more than a year—to see a specialist, to have elective surgery like hip replacements or to get radiation treatment for cancer. All told, 827,429 people are waiting for some type of procedure in Canada. In England, nearly 1.8 million people are waiting for a hospital admission or outpatient treatment.

Fact No. 7: People in countries with more government control of health care are highly dissatisfied and believe reform is needed. More than 70 percent of German, Canadian, Australian, New Zealand and British adults say their health system needs either "fundamental change" or "complete rebuilding."

Fact No. 8: Americans are more satisfied with the care they receive than Canadians. When asked about their own health care instead of the "health care system," more than half of Americans (51.3 percent) are very satisfied with their health care services, compared to only 41.5 percent of Canadians; a lower proportion of Americans are dissatisfied (6.8 percent) than Canadians (8.5 percent).

Despite serious challenges ... the U.S. health care system compares favorably to those in other developed countries.

American Medical Innovation

Fact No. 9: Americans have much better access to important new technologies like medical imaging than patients in Canada or the U.K. Maligned as a waste by economists and policy makers naïve to actual medical practice, an overwhelming majority of leading American physicians identified computerized tomography (CT) and magnetic resonance imaging (MRI) as the most important medical innovations for improving patient care during the previous decade. The United States has 34 CT scanners per million Americans, compared to 12 in Canada and eight in Britain. The United States has nearly 27 MRI machines per million compared to about 6 per million in Canada and Britain.

Fact No. 10: Americans are responsible for the vast majority of all health care innovations. The top five U.S. hospitals conduct more clinical trials than all the hospitals in any other single developed country. Since the mid-1970s, the Nobel Prize in medicine or physiology has gone to American residents more often than recipients from all other countries combined. In only five of the past 34 years did a scientist living in America not win or share in the prize. Most important recent medical innovations were developed in the United States.

Despite serious challenges, such as escalating costs and the uninsured, the U.S. health care system compares favorably to those in other developed countries.

The Health Care Experience in France Is Better than in the United States

Matt Welch

In the following viewpoint, Matt Welch argues that the quality of health care in France is better in many respects than in the United States. Welch contends that because the French health care system covers everyone with little bureaucracy, it is easier, faster, and less expensive to see a high-quality doctor in France. Although Welch does not endorse the French model of socialized medicine, he concludes that the US system—by being a hybrid between public and private—has been failing for a long time and is overdue for change. Welch is editor in chief of Reason *magazine.*

As you read, consider the following questions:

1. According to Welch, the French health care system is better than the US health care system on what three counts?

2. What particular demographic does the author claim is likely better off with the US health care system?

3. Welch claims he was denied health insurance as a freelancer for what reason?

Matt Welch, "Why I Prefer French Health Care," *Reason*, vol. 41, no. 8, January 2010, pp. 2–3. Copyright © 2010 Reason Magazine and Reason.com. All rights reserved. Reproduced by permission.

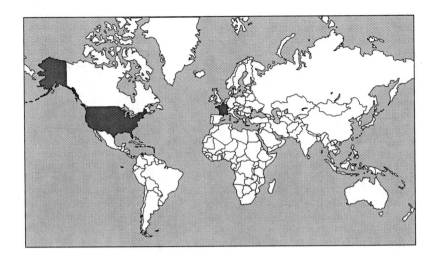

By now I'm accustomed to being the only person in any given room with my particular set of cockamamie politics. But even within the more familiar confines of the libertarian movement, I am an awkward outlier on the topic of the day: health care.

To put it plainly, when free marketers warn that Democratic health care initiatives will make us more "like France," a big part of me says, "I wish." It's not that I think it's either feasible or advisable for the United States to adopt a single-payer, government-dominated system. But it's instructive to confront the comparative advantages of one socialist system abroad to sharpen the arguments for more capitalism at home.

The French Health Care System

For a dozen years now I've led a dual life, spending more than 90 percent of my time and money in the U.S. while receiving 90 percent of my health care in my wife's native France. On a personal level the comparison is no contest: I'll take the French experience any day. ObamaCare opponents often warn that a new system will lead to long waiting times, mountains of paperwork, and less choice among doctors. Yet on all three of those counts the French system is significantly *better*, not worse, than what the U.S. has now.

Need a prescription for muscle relaxers, an antifungal cream, or a steroid inhaler for temporary lung trouble? In the U.S. you have to fight to get on the appointment schedule of a doctor within your health insurance network (I'll conservatively put the average wait time at five days), then have him or her scrawl something unintelligible on a slip of paper, which you take to a drugstore to exchange for your medicine. You might pay the doc $40, but then his office sends you a separate bill for the visit, and for an examination, and those bills also go to your insurance company, which sends you an adjustment sheet weeks after the doctor's office has sent its third payment notice. By the time it's all sorted out, you've probably paid a few hundred dollars to three different entities, without having a clue about how or why any of the prices were set.

It's instructive to confront the comparative advantages of one socialist system abroad to sharpen the arguments for more capitalism at home.

In France, by contrast, you walk to the corner pharmacist, get either a prescription or over-the-counter medication right away, shell out a dozen or so euros, and you're done. If you need a doctor, it's not hard to get an appointment within a day or three, you make payments for everything (including X-rays) on the spot, and the amounts are routinely less than the co-payments for U.S. doctor visits. I've had back X-rays, detailed ear examinations, even minor oral surgery, and never have I paid more than maybe €300 for any one procedure.

The Temptation of Socialized Medicine

And it's not like the medical professionals in France are chopped liver. In the U.S., my wife had some lumps in her breast dismissed as harmless by a hurried, indifferent doctor at Kaiser Permanente. Eight months later, during our annual Christmas visit in Lyon, one of the best breast surgeons in the country detected that the lumps were growing and removed them.

We know that the horrific amount of third-party gobble-dygook in America, the cost insensitivity, and the price randomness are all products of bad policies that market reforms could significantly improve. We know, too, that France's low retail costs are subsidized by punitively high tax rates that will have to increase unless benefits are cut. If you are rich and sick (or a healthy doctor), you're likely better off here. But as long as the U.S. remains this ungainly public-private hybrid, with ever-tighter mandates producing ever-fewer consumer choices, the average consumer's health care experience will probably be more pleasing in France.

As long as the U.S. remains this ungainly public-private hybrid . . . the average consumer's health care experience will probably be more pleasing in France.

What's more, none of these anecdotes scratches the surface of France's chief advantage, and the main reason socialized medicine remains a perennial temptation in this country: In France, you are covered, period. It doesn't depend on your job, it doesn't depend on a health maintenance organization, and it doesn't depend on whether you filled out the paperwork right. Those who (like me) oppose ObamaCare, need to understand (also like me, unfortunately) what it's like to be serially rejected by insurance companies even though you're perfectly healthy. It's an enraging, anxiety-inducing, indelible experience, one that both softens the intellectual ground for increased government intervention and produces active resentment toward anyone who argues that the U.S. has "the best health care in the world."

A Struggle with Health Insurance

Since 1986 I've missed exactly three days of work due to illness. I don't smoke, I don't (usually) do drugs or drink to excess, and I eat a pretty healthy diet. I have some back pain now and then from a protruding disc, but nothing too serious. And from 1998 to 2001, when I was a freelancer in the world's capital of freelancers (Los Angeles), I couldn't get health insurance.

Kaiser rejected me because I had visited the doctor too many times in the 12 months preceding my application (I filled in the "3–5 times" circle, to reflect the three routine and inexpensive checkups I'd had in France). Blue Cross rejected me too. There weren't many other options. Months later, an insurance broker told me I'd mined my chances by failing to file a written appeal. "You're basically done in California," he said. "A rejection is like an arrest—if you don't contest it, you're guilty, and it's on your permanent record."

Are we better off today, in terms of health policy, than we would have been had we acknowledged more loudly 15 years ago that the status quo is quite awful for a large number of Americans?

It wasn't as if I wanted or needed to consume much health care then. I was in my early 30s, and I wanted to make sure a catastrophic illness or injury wouldn't bankrupt my family. When I finally found a freelance-journalist collective that allowed me and my wife to pay $212 a month to hedge against a car accident, it a) refused to cover pregnancies or childbirths at any price and b) hiked the monthly rate up to $357 after a year. One of the main attractions of moving from freelance status to a full-time job was the ability to affix a stable price on my health insurance.

U.S. Health Care Solutions

This is the exact opposite of the direction in which we should be traveling in a global just-in-time economy, with its ideal of entrepreneurial workers breaking free of corporate command and zipping creatively from project to project. Don't even get me started on the Kafkaesque [nightmarishly complex or illogical] ordeal of switching jobs without taking any time off, yet going uncovered by anything except COBRA for nearly two months, even though both employers used the same health insurance provider. That incident alone cost me thousands of dollars I wouldn't have paid if I had controlled my own insurance policy.

I've now reached the age where I will better appreciate the premium skill level of American doctors and their high-quality equipment and techniques. And in a very real way my family has voted with its feet when it comes to choosing between the two countries. One of France's worst problems is the rigidity and expense that comes with an extensive welfare state.

But as you look at the health care solutions . . . ask yourself an honest question: Are we better off today, in terms of health policy, than we would have been had we acknowledged more loudly 15 years ago that the status quo is quite awful for a large number of Americans? Would we have been better off focusing less on waiting times in Britain, and more on waiting times in the USA? It's a question I plan to ask my doctor this Christmas. In French.

The National Health Service in Great Britain Needs Reform

Spectator (UK)

In the following viewpoint, the Spectator, a weekly online and print magazine in the United Kingdom that focuses on political and current events, argues that Britain's single-payer health care system, the National Health Service (NHS), is in dire need of improvement. The Spectator contends that although the goal of universal health care is a good one that has wide support, the current system of providing health care is economically unsustainable. The Spectator claims that the current government monopoly of the system, along with the irrelevance of cost to users, needs to be considered in a serious reformation of the current NHS.

As you read, consider the following questions:

1. According to the *Spectator*, Great Britain's National Health Service (NHS) was founded in what decade?

2. Although the *Spectator* grants that state-funded health care is not going away, it denies that logic dictates that the state should play what role?

3. According to the author, what percentage of the billions invested in the NHS in 2004/05 went to pensions?

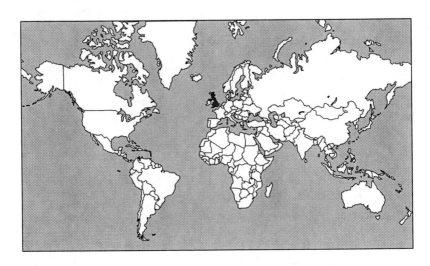

The [British] government has promised that from next year [2009] everyone aged between 40 and 75 will be offered an 'MOT' [full health screening] of their health. The patient most in need of a health check, however, was 60 this week: the NHS [National Health Service] itself. To a limited extent the government has recognised the inadequacies of what for its first three or so decades tended to be called 'the envy of the world' by using the anniversary to publish the NHS next stage review, written by Lord Darzi, a junior health minister and eminent surgeon. The document is less celebratory than defensive, effectively admitting that the patient has often become lost in an organisation which is one of the world's largest employers after China's Red Army. Sadly, much of what it goes on to propose will, in fact, entrench that very bureaucracy.

The National Health Service

At the outset, one should recognise what is good about the NHS. The principle of universal healthcare for all, regardless of the patient's ability to pay, caught the public's imagination in the 1940s, gave institutional expression to the social solidarity of the war years, and remains dear to patients to this day. While Britain had some excellent hospitals in 1948, many

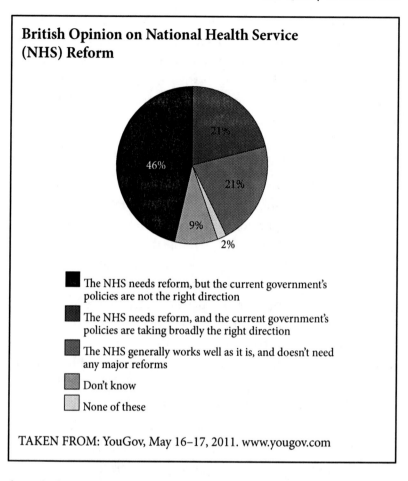

British Opinion on National Health Service (NHS) Reform

- The NHS needs reform, but the current government's policies are not the right direction
- The NHS needs reform, and the current government's policies are taking broadly the right direction
- The NHS generally works well as it is, and doesn't need any major reforms
- Don't know
- None of these

TAKEN FROM: YouGov, May 16–17, 2011. www.yougov.com

founded with generous benefactions, getting into them was not easy for all. The foundation of the NHS happened to coincide with the introduction of antibiotics, which, combined with improvements in hygiene, sent infectious diseases in Britain into rapid decline.

It is no accident that the NHS survived the privatisations of the 1980s and is still supported by the Conservatives today. [British politician] Nigel Lawson's famous remark that the health service was the closest thing the English had to a religion was correct. Yet—to extend the metaphor—the flock is growing querulous at the management of the church. According to a YouGov poll in the *Daily Telegraph* this week [June

23–25, 2008], only 21 per cent look forward to any real improvement in the NHS; 78 per cent think there are too many managers; and 82 per cent believe that 'a great deal' or a 'fair amount' of money is wasted in the health service. If the NHS is a religion, it is badly in need of a Martin Luther figure and a root-and-branch Reformation.

Attempts at Reformation

The principle of universal, state-funded healthcare remains more or less sacrosanct. It does not follow that the state should be the monopoly provider. Rightly, if belatedly, the government has experimented with making the NHS a buyer of private services. Unfortunately, not all these experiments have been a success, often because of bureaucratic ineptitude or cultural hostility towards the private sector within the NHS: Private companies offering hernia treatments, for example, have been given contracts ensuring they were paid no matter how few patients chose their services. And why is that? All too frequently because GPs [general practitioners] have been reluctant to make referrals to private treatment centres.

If the NHS is a religion, it is badly in need of a Martin Luther figure and a root-and-branch Reformation.

Lord Darzi now proposes that hospitals be penalised financially for failing their patients. Fine in theory, but we know what happens in practice when public bodies are fined for transgressions: The taxpayer merely ends up paying the fine. More promising is a proposal to give patients an individual budget for their treatment—which they can spend in different ways. For the first time, then, NHS patients will be able to appreciate the real cost of their treatment—and perhaps be disabused of the delusion that state services are 'free'. As the state of the public finances deteriorates and taxpayers feel the pinch, it is more important than ever that the public debate about tax-and-spend rise above its present infantilized level. Voters and politicians need to hold a mature dialogue about value for money and the proper limits of public expenditure: This dialogue has been scandalously postponed by New Labour's pretence that its so-called 'investment' in the public services has been a 'gift' from government to people, rather than a drain on the public's own resources.

The Rising Cost of Care

Along with the rise in hospital infections, the lack of cost control within the NHS is this government's biggest failure in health policy. In 2002, Gordon Brown, then chancellor, accepted a proposal from Sir Derek Wanless that healthcare spending be doubled by 2022 to bring it in line with health spending in other European countries—putting a penny on National Insurance in order to pay for it. What he didn't say was what he intended to achieve with the money; rather, spending was adjudged to be a good in itself, intrinsically virtuous. Small wonder, then, that of the extra £5 billion put into the NHS in 2004/05 alone a mere 2.4 per cent went on operations and new beds—while 27 per cent went on pay rises and 29 per cent on pensions.

Left to its own devices, the NHS would quite happily grow into a monster which would consume all Britain's wealth. As John Appleby, chief economist of the healthcare think tank the King's Fund, points out: At current rates of expansion by 2046 the NHS would account for one in every two pounds spent in Britain. And yet—even then—we would not be assured of better healthcare: Spending in this area is subject to a law of diminishing returns, where huge sums are spent extending the lives of terminally ill patients by a few days.

The biggest failure of the [Prime Minister Clement Richard] Attlee government when constituting the NHS in 1948 was to detach healthcare from economic reality and to fail to give the new service any defined boundaries. It is about time such limits were honestly discussed. Rationing is a daily reality in the NHS, but not one that is properly acknowledged. And how are we to reconcile the public's desire for the devolution of control to communities and individuals with its equal distaste for the 'postcode lottery'? Everyone says they want to move beyond the 'one-size-fits-all' ethos of the NHS to a structure of greater diversity and variety; and yet there is still an insistence upon uniform standards. Clearly, this debate is in its very infancy.

Left to its own devices, the NHS would quite happily grow into a monster which would consume all Britain's wealth.

Of all nationalised institutions, the NHS looks the safest: No party has the slightest intention of dismantling it or privatising it. We regret that the Conservative Party's position on healthcare is so timid. Lord Darzi is not the Martin Luther–style reformer that the health service needs; but nor, on present evidence, is [leader of the Conservative Party] David Cameron.

Cuba's Health Care System Works Well in Cuba and Elsewhere

Sarah van Gelder

In the following viewpoint, Sarah van Gelder argues that not only is the quality of health care in Cuba working well, but Cuba is also exporting its health care all over the world. Cuba not only sends its doctors to many parts of the world to provide medical care, according to van Gelder, Cuba also trains thousands of medical students from all over the world, with a focus on training medical professionals to work with the poor. Van Gelder claims that Cuba's medical aid missions and medical training have been an investment in peace for the country, helping it to forge alliances with many other nations. Van Gelder is cofounder and executive editor of YES! *magazine.*

As you read, consider the following questions:

1. According to van Gelder, Cubans are as healthy as those in the wealthiest countries with what important difference?

2. How many foreign students attend Havana's Latin American School of Medicine, according to the author?

3. According to van Gelder, how many Cuban health professionals are practicing medicine abroad?

Sarah van Gelder, "Health Care for All. Love, Cuba" *Yes!*, no. 42, Summer 2007. yesmagazine.org.

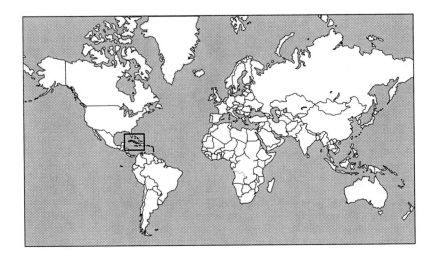

Cubans say they offer health care to the world's poor because they have big hearts. But what do they get in return?

They live longer than almost anyone in Latin America. Far fewer babies die. Almost everyone has been vaccinated, and such scourges of the poor as parasites, TB [tuberculosis], malaria, even HIV/AIDS are rare or nonexistent. Anyone can see a doctor, at low cost, right in the neighborhood.

The Health Care System of Cuba

The Cuban health care system is producing a population that is as healthy as those of the world's wealthiest countries at a fraction of the cost. And now Cuba has begun exporting its system to underserved communities around the world—including the United States.

The story of Cuba's health care ambitions is largely hidden from the people of the United States, where politics left over from the Cold War maintain an embargo on information and understanding. But it is increasingly well known in the poorest communities of Latin America, the Caribbean, and parts of Africa where Cuban and Cuban-trained doctors are practicing.

In the words of Dr. Paul Farmer, Cuba is showing that "you can introduce the notion of a right to health care and wipe out the diseases of poverty."

Many elements of the health care system Cuba is exporting around the world are commonsense practices. Everyone has access to doctors, nurses, specialists, and medications. There is a doctor and nurse team in every neighborhood, although somewhat fewer now, with 29,000 medical professionals serving out of the country—a fact that is causing some complaints. If someone doesn't like their neighborhood doctor, they can choose another one.

The Cuban health care system is producing a population that is as healthy as those of the world's wealthiest countries at a fraction of the cost.

House calls are routine, in part because it's the responsibility of the doctor and nurse team to understand you and your health issues in the context of your family, home, and neighborhood. This is key to the system. By catching diseases and health hazards before they get big, the Cuban medical system can spend a little on prevention rather than a lot later on to cure diseases, stop outbreaks, or cope with long-term disabilities. When a health hazard like dengue fever or malaria is identified, there is a coordinated nationwide effort to eradicate it. Cubans no longer suffer from diphtheria, rubella, polio, or measles and they have the lowest AIDS rate in the Americas, and the highest rate of treatment and control of hypertension.

For health issues beyond the capacity of the neighborhood doctor, polyclinics provide specialists, outpatient operations, physical therapy, rehabilitation, and labs. Those who need inpatient treatment can go to hospitals; at the end of their stay, their neighborhood medical team helps make the transition home. Doctors at all levels are trained to administer acupuncture, herbal cures, or other complementary practices that Cuban labs have found effective. And Cuban researchers develop their own vaccinations and treatments when medications aren't available due to the blockade, or when they don't exist.

Cuba's Medical Training Program

For decades, Cuba has sent doctors abroad and trained international students at its medical schools. But things ramped up beginning in 1998 when Hurricanes George and Mitch hammered Central America and the Caribbean. As they had often done, Cuban doctors rushed to the disaster zone to help those suffering the aftermath. But when it was time to go home, it was clear to the Cuban teams that the medical needs extended far beyond emergency care. So Cuba made a commitment to post doctors in several of these countries and to train local people in medicine so they could pick up where the Cuban doctors left off. ELAM, the Havana-based Latin American School of Medicine, was born, and with it the offer of 10,000 scholarships for free medical training.

Today the program has grown to 22,000 students from Latin America, the Caribbean, Africa, Asia, and the United States who attend ELAM and 28 other medical schools across Cuba. The students represent dozens of ethnic groups, 51 percent are women, and they come from more than 30 countries. What they have in common is that they would otherwise be unable to get a medical education. When a slum dweller in Port-au-Prince, a young indigenous person from Bolivia, the son or daughter of a farmer in Honduras, or a street vendor in the Gambia wants to become a doctor, they turn to Cuba. In some cases, Venezuela pays the bill. But most of the time, Cuba covers tuition, living expenses, books, and medical care. In return, the students agree that, upon completion of their studies, they will return to their own underserved communities to practice medicine.

The curriculum at ELAM begins, for most students, with up to a year of "bridging" courses, allowing them to catch up on basic math, science, and Spanish skills. The students are treated for the ailments many bring with them.

At the end of their training, which can take up to eight years, most students return home for residencies. Although they all make a verbal commitment to serve the poor, a few students quietly admit that they don't see this as a permanent commitment.

For decades, Cuba has sent doctors abroad and trained international students at its medical schools.

One challenge of the Cuban approach is making sure their investment in medical education benefits those who need it most. Doctors from poor areas routinely move to wealthier areas or out of the country altogether. Cuba trains doctors in an ethic of serving the poor. They learn to see medical care as a right, not as a commodity, and to see their own role as one of service. Stories of Cuban doctors who practice abroad suggest these lessons stick. They are known for taking money out of their own pockets to buy medicine for patients who can't afford to fill a prescription, and for touching and even embracing patients.

Cuba plans with the help of Venezuela to take their medical training to a massive scale and graduate 100,000 doctors over the next 15 years, according to Dr. Juan Ceballos, advisor to the vice minister of public health. To do so, Cuba has been building new medical schools around the country and abroad, at a rapid clip.

But the scale of the effort required to address current and projected needs for doctors requires breaking out of the box. The new approach is medical schools without walls. Students meet their teachers in clinics and hospitals, in Cuba and abroad, practicing alongside their mentors. Videotaped lectures and training software mean students can study anywhere there are Cuban doctors. The lower training costs make possible a scale of medical education that could end the scarcity of doctors.

Cuba's Relationship with the United States

Recently, Cuba extended the offer of free medical training to students from the United States. It started when Representative Bennie Thompson of Mississippi got curious after he and other members of the Congressional Black Caucus repeatedly encountered Cuban or Cuban-trained doctors in poor communities around the world.

They visited Cuba in May 2000, and during a conversation with [then president] Fidel Castro, Thompson brought up the lack of medical access for his poor, rural constituents. "He [Castro] was very familiar with the unemployment rates, health conditions, and infant mortality rates in my district, and that surprised me," Thompson said. Castro offered scholarships for low-income Americans under the same terms as the other international students—they have to agree to go back and serve their communities.

Today, about 90 young people from poor parts of the United States have joined the ranks of international students studying medicine in Cuba.

The offer of medical training is just one way Cuba has reached out to the United States. Immediately after Hurricanes Katrina and Rita, 1,500 Cuban doctors volunteered to come to the Gulf Coast. They waited with packed bags and medical supplies, and a ship ready to provide backup support. Permission from the U.S. government never arrived.

"Our government played politics with the lives of people when they needed help the most," said Representative Thompson. "And that's unfortunate."

Cuba's Missions Abroad

When an earthquake struck Pakistan shortly afterwards, though, that country's government warmly welcomed the Cuban medical professionals. And 2,300 came, bringing 32 field hospitals to remote, frigid regions of the Himalayas. There, they set broken bones, treated ailments, and performed operations for a total of 1.7 million patients.

About 90 young people from poor parts of the United States have joined the ranks of international students studying medicine in Cuba.

The disaster assistance is part of Cuba's medical aid mission that has extended from Peru to Indonesia, and even included caring for 17,000 children sickened by the 1986 accident at the Chernobyl nuclear plant in the Ukraine.

It isn't only in times of disaster that Cuban health care workers get involved. Some 29,000 Cuban health professionals are now practicing in 69 countries—mostly in Latin America, the Caribbean, and Africa. In Venezuela, about 20,000 of them have enabled President Hugo Chávez to make good on his promise to provide health care to the poor. In the shantytowns around Caracas and the banks of the Amazon, those who organize themselves and find a place for a doctor to practice and live can request a Cuban doctor.

As in Cuba, these doctors and nurses live where they serve, and become part of the community. They are available for emergencies, and they introduce preventative health practices.

Some are tempted to use their time abroad as an opportunity to leave Cuba. In August, the U.S. Department of Homeland Security announced a new policy that makes it easier for Cuban medical professionals to come to the U.S. But the vast majority remain on the job and eventually return to Cuba.

An Investment in Peace

How do the Cuban people feel about using their country's resources for international medical missions? Those I asked responded with some version of this: We Cubans have big hearts. We are proud that we can share what we have with the world's poor.

Nearly everyone in Cuba knows someone who has served on a medical mission. These doctors encounter maladies that have been eradicated from Cuba. They expand their understanding of medicine and of the suffering associated with poverty and powerlessness, and they bring home the pride that goes with making a difference.

And pride is a potent antidote to the dissatisfaction that can result from the economic hardships that continue 50 years into Cuba's revolution.

Some 29,000 Cuban health professionals are now practicing in 69 countries—mostly in Latin America, the Caribbean, and Africa.

From the government's perspective, their investment in medical internationalism is covered, in part, by ALBA, the new trade agreement among Venezuela, Bolivia, Nicaragua and Cuba. ALBA, an alternative to the free trade area of the Americas, puts human needs ahead of economic growth, so it isn't surprising that Cuba's health care offerings fall within the agreement, as does Venezuelan oil, Bolivian natural gas, and so on. But Cuba also offers help to countries outside of ALBA.

"All we ask for in return is solidarity," Dr. Ceballos says.

"Solidarity" has real-world implications. Before Cuba sent doctors to Pakistan, relations between the two countries were not great, Ceballos says. But now the relationship is "magnificent." The same is true of Guatemala and El Salvador. "Although they are conservative governments, they have become more flexible in their relationship with Cuba," he says.

Those investments in health care missions "are resources that prevent confrontation with other nations," Ceballos explains. "The solidarity with Cuba has restrained aggressions of all kinds." And in a statement that acknowledges Cuba's vulnerabilities on the global stage, Ceballos puts it this way: "It's infinitely better to invest in peace than to invest in war."

Imagine, then, that this idea took hold. Even more revolutionary than the right to health care for all is the idea that an investment in health—or in clean water, adequate food or housing—could be more powerful, more effective at building security than bombers and aircraft carriers.

Beyond Hysterics: The Health Care Model That Works

Anita Raghavan

In the following viewpoint, Anita Raghavan contends that Germany's mix of private and public health insurance plans leads to a high-quality health care system with much lower costs than in the United States. Raghavan claims that the vast majority of Germans are insured through the public system and most are happy with their health care. However, she notes that some doctors and pharmaceutical companies do not like the system because of its strict cost controls. She concludes that fears of a two-tier system have not materialized in Germany, but she says that there are looming challenges for Germany as medical costs continue to rise. Raghavan is a reporter and acting London bureau chief for Forbes *magazine.*

As you read, consider the following questions:

1. According to Raghavan, what percentage of the German population has chosen the public insurance system?

2. The German public insurance system is financed by a payroll tax that amounts to what portion of a person's salary, according to Raghavan?

3. According to the author, what percentage of the German population with a chronic condition reported paying more than $1,000 in health costs in the past year?

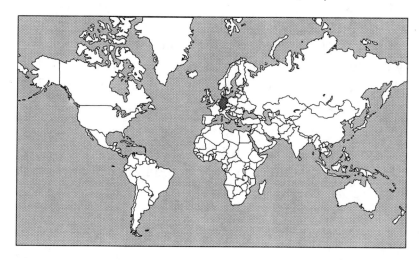

As a young man working for Suhrkamp Verlag, the renowned publishing house in Berlin, Michael Prolingheuer bought private health insurance. Coverage was then relatively cheap (though it now costs $905 a month). It also promised greater choice of doctors and easier access to care than Germany's statutory quasi-public plan, which consists of 187 nonprofit insurers closely supervised, but not run, by the government.

Today, 28 years later, he's having second thoughts. In January 2007 Prolingheuer, now 54, was diagnosed with amyotrophic lateral sclerosis (also known as Lou Gehrig's disease), a progressive disease of the nervous system that paralyzes and ultimately kills a patient. Not long after he got the grim news, the fight with his insurer began. At first his carrier, Allianz, balked at paying for the respirator that helps him breathe, arguing it wasn't specified in his policy. It only relented after a doctor at Berlin's Charité-Universitätsmedizin, a teaching hospital, sent a letter saying that without the machine he would die. Then Allianz suggested cutting the amount of time Prolingheuer was hooked up to the respirator, which would lower treatment costs by eliminating round-the-clock home nurses. In a letter dated June 10, 2009, it asked him for a medical report that would state "to what extent your daily breathing treatment could be reduced to heighten your quality of life" and inquired to what degree his wife assisted him in his daily routine, as "she has been trained in using these machines."

"We deeply regret causing Mr. Prolingheuer distress," says an Allianz spokesperson. She adds that while his policy "does not cover the particular medical equipment he requested, Allianz nevertheless provided it after confirming with his m.d. that this was needed."

Prolingheuer isn't having any of it. "My insurer would like to see me dead," he taps out on his black laptop. Lying in a short-sleeve black sports shirt and striped pajama bottoms, Prolingheuer can no longer speak and is mostly confined to his bed. He paid insurance premiums for many years. "Now that I need the basic care, they say no." He figures his care costs as much as $370,000 a year, of which his out-of-pocket cost is $21,000 in addition to his monthly premiums. If he had to do it over again, Prolingheuer says, he would be part of Germany's public insurance system—the choice of 90% of the population, 74 million or so people.

Whether they have public or private coverage, most Germans love their care.

People like Angela Jansen, 53. Diagnosed with ALS in March 1995, her care is covered by public insurer Barmer, which, together with the government, pays $360,000 or so a year to support round-the-clock nurses. Jansen, too, can no longer speak or use her hands and legs but relies on a computer with a laser camera that captures the movements of her left pupil as it scans letters on the keyboard. "This thing called Eyegaze the insurer paid for, the wheelchair, the breathing machines . . . the things I need to live," she writes. Where it skimps: on medicines, offering generics, which "are not always the best. Sure I get what's on the list, but not everything is on it," she writes. One excluded item is a cream that might prevent her bedsores.

This pair of patients with extreme needs represents the two faces of health care in Germany and its mix of private and quasi-public insurance plans. More than any model in the world, the German system offers a glimpse of what health care could look like in the U.S. That's assuming any bill survives the popular revolt. Unlike many countries with national health—Canada, say, or the U.K.—where private insurance generally supplements public coverage, Germany has two separate systems that coexist, with private plans indirectly benefiting from the cost controls of the public system.

Whether they have public or private coverage, most Germans love their care. In a recent survey by M&M Management & Marketing Consulting, 84% of private insurance clients expressed satisfaction; so did 85% of those who rely on the public system. Tough to find that in America. Germany spends $3,588 per capita, per year, or 10.4% of its GDP, on health care. The U.S. shells out $7,290 per person, 16% of economic output. This difference is not because we have more old people. One in five Germans is 65 or older, compared with one in eight in the U.S.

"If you want a health care system where you don't have to worry that you could go broke, where you could lose your health insurance or get off-the-charts doctors bills, look at the German model," says Uwe Reinhardt, economics professor at Princeton University. He believes that German and Swiss systems, which offer near-universal care without rationing services, come closest to something that Americans, long used to a private system, could stomach.

The two-pronged approach dates to 1883, when Chancellor Otto von Bismarck created a way to provide health care to industrial workers, with the cost shared between employers and employees. Since then the system has expanded, eclipsing the private model of health care, which dominated the early 20th century. Today health care is virtually universal. An estimated 200,000 residents, including guest workers and the self-employed, escape the net, usually because they can't afford basic coverage. Their penalty for failing to enroll is only that they have to pay back premiums if they seek medical help.

In Germany private repayment . . . is always more generous than what is dished out by the public system.

This is close to, but not fully, socialized medicine. The public insurance system is largely financed by a payroll tax amounting to 14.9% of a person's salary, with employees picking up 7.9% and employers taking the rest. As for disability, employers pay six weeks' salary; after that the sickness fund, or nonprofit insurer, pays 80%, subject to a cap, for 18 months. This year the government will kick in an additional $10.3 billion to help cover children, maternity benefits and home help. Unemployment insurance pays the fees for those out of a job. Premiums in the public system are based on income and not an individual's risk (that is, age and current health). It's a different story for those with private insurance, where high-risk people pay higher premiums. There are sometimes deductibles in the private system, but public patients have only co-pays.

How does Germany do it? By doing what Medicare does and more. It sets fixed reimbursement rates for hospitals and wields a stick Medicare lacks: extracting price concessions from drug companies. But Germany's quasi-public system has more leverage because it accounts for a larger share of medical spending (albeit the power of the purse is dispersed among 16 states). German general practitioners earn $80,000 or more a year, with three-fourths of their gross income coming from publicly insured patients. In the U.S. general practitioners (including family physicians) gross an average $161,490. In

German vs. American Health Care

	GERMANY	U.S.
Percentage of GDP Spent on Health Care	10.4%	16%
Health Care Spending per Capita	$3,588	$7,290
Average Annual Growth Rate of Real Health Care Spending per Capita 1997-2007	1.7%	3.4%
Out-of-Pocket Health Care Spending per Capita	$470	$890
Per Capita Spending on Health Insurance[1]	$191	$516
Per Capita Spending on Drugs[1]	$542	$878
Number of Practicing Doctors per 1,000	3.5	2.4
Average Annual Number of Doctor Visits	7.5	3.8[2]
Average Length of Stay for Acute Care	7.8	5.5

[1] Adjusted for cost-of-living differences. [2] 2006.
Source: Organisation for Economic Co-operation & Development.

TAKEN FROM: Anita Raghavan, "Beyond Hysterics: The Health Care Model That Works," *Forbes*, September 21, 2009. www.forbes.com.

Germany private repayment, though, is always more generous than what is dished out by the public system. Some specialists say in their ads that they will treat only higher-paying private patients. As a result, the patients who are on the private system and don't have unusual conditions like ALS often get access to better doctors.

Eva Czerep, a general practitioner in one of Berlin's poorest neighborhoods, says she gets a lump sum $50 per patient per quarter, no matter how many visits they make. Extra treatments don't always bring sizable fees. Paging through two thick books of different reimbursement rates for public and private patients, Czerep says she can collect an additional $7 to $10 by giving a publicly insured patient a flu shot; blood tests bring in nothing extra. (By contrast, taking blood from a private patient pulls in $8; a flu vaccine, $29). "A plumber earns more money fixing a washing machine than I do in an hour treating a patient," Czerep complains.

As a GP, Czerep says she must keep within a fixed budget for medications. If she overshoots it, she might have to switch to, say, cheaper insulin shots. Exceed her budget and she has to refund the government roughly 10% of the cost overrun, she says. (That's never happened.) To avoid such situations, some doctors go on holiday the last week of a quarter. A Health Ministry spokesman says "there is no fixed budget" for drugs, but he concedes if a doctor "does not prescribe drugs efficiently and economically, she may have to pay back money."

Collective bargaining keeps drug prices lower than they are in the States. One hundred 75-milligram tablets of Plavix, the blood thinner, cost $400 in Germany and $478 in the U.S.; 100-milligram tablets of Seroquel, which treats schizophrenia and bipolar disorder, cost roughly half as much in Germany as they do on Drugstore.com. Pricing policies sometimes spark controversy. Pfizer, for example, has been contesting a decision by German authorities to cap the amount public insurers are willing to pay for Lipitor (which retails for $55 a month in Germany, compared with $125 in the U.S.). Patients must cover the difference between retail prices and the amount public insurers cover. As a result of the gap, Pfizer has claimed in a pending suit that the number of publicly insured Germans using its best-selling anticholesterol drug fell to 250,000 in 2005, from 1.5 million at the end of 2004.

Another cost container: Germany's hospitals don't splurge like inebriated mariners on the latest technology. Two years ago the nation had 8 magnetic resonance imaging machines and 16 computed tomography scanners per 1 million people, compared with 26 MRIs and 34 CTs in the U.S., reports the Organisation for Economic Co-operation and Development. Because there are low numbers of uninsured patients, fewer Germans rely on expensive emergency room care to replace a cheap office visit. According to a survey by the Commonwealth Fund, a New York City health care research foundation, only 6% of Germans with a chronic condition (heart disease, diabetes or cancer, among others) use the ER for something treatable by a regular doctor—the lowest rate in Europe and far lower than the 19% rate among those surveyed in the U.S.

Helping to slow costs, the German government has for a number of years nudged its citizens into the public system by raising the income threshold ... for private insurance.

For a full hip replacement—from initial consultation to a hospital stay of seven to ten days for surgery and post-op— Charité-Universitätsmedizin receives $9,700 for a young and healthy patient, and $11,050 for someone old and infirm, when both have public insurance. Private reimbursement for each group can run twice as much, says professor Carsten Perka, Charité's orthopedic chief.

Helping to slow costs, the German government has for a number of years nudged its citizens into the public system by raising the income threshold (at least $70,000 a year for three consecutive years) for private insurance. Net new private enrollments came to 59,900 in 2007, an almost 50% decrease from 2006. To stop the drain on the public system as people get older and need more care, the government bars anyone 55 years or older with private care from switching back to public.

One of the primal fears about reform in the U.S.—that it would create a two-tier system where privately insured patients would get better care and shorter waits—is largely a nonissue in Germany. The public system is so dominant that when it comes to the treatment of chronic illnesses, it matches and, in some cases, beats the care available with private coverage. As for long delays in treatment, 68% of public and private patients surveyed by the Commonwealth Fund reported waiting less than four weeks to see a specialist, compared with 74% in the U.S. (Sometimes patients with public insurance must wait longer for appointments.) The German system scored high, too, when it came to out-of-pocket expenses: Only 13% of those with a chronic condition reported spending more than $1,000 in the past year, compared with 41% in the U.S.

"I personally would prefer for the private system to die," says Karl Lauterbach, professor of health economics and epidemiology at the University of Cologne. As a member of the Bundestag, Germany's parliament, Lauterbach has been at the forefront of efforts to tighten eligibility in the private system. "Why should I care about a system that is more costly, less efficient and is even a problem for patients in the system?"

One of the primal fears about reform in the U.S. . . . is largely a nonissue in Germany.

He'd get no argument from Hartmut Sinapius, a 62-year-old self-employed criminal defense lawyer. In July he checked into Charité's orthopedic ward to change the hip replacement on his left side—his sixth operation. Sinapius pays $750 a month, reflecting a high salary, to Allgemeine Ortskranken-

kasse, or local health fund, the largest social insurance provider in Germany. He kicks in an additional $115 a month for
private insurance, which buys him his own room and treatment by orthopedic chief Perka when he is hospitalized. "Privately you pay a lot more as you get older," says Sinapius. But
without the extra premium he pays, "I wouldn't have that
pretty picture on the wall."

In fact, he would. On the same floor a few doors down
Andrea Staack, 40, shares with another public patient an iden-
tical room with a similar framed photo. A home-health aide,
Staack each year takes home $13,730—and collects $4,580 in
government benefits to support her child. While her care has
been first rate, she's not under Perka's supervision.

---

*The state, once willing to lavish money on medical care,
has turned tightfisted.*

When her hip started hurting last year, Staack came directly to Charité, where doctors suggested surgery. Alarmed at
the idea, she settled for an interim step this year: an arthros-
copy. She was admitted to Park-Klinik Weissensee, a private
state-of-the-art clinic in northern Berlin that takes both public and private patients. "It was like a resort," she says. Since
there were ample beds, she had her own room and stayed for
a few days. But soon after she was released her pain was worse
than before. Because of a cancelation, she managed to schedule an operation at Charité within three weeks. "Normally it
would have taken six weeks," she says.

For all her medical care this year, including her stays at
Charité and Park-Klinik, plus drug and transportation costs to
the hospital, Staack will pay $61. As a public patient she
couldn't choose her surgeon; her insurer closely prescribes her
care. After her April operation Staack wanted special plasters
with painkillers embedded in them, but her insurer wouldn't
pay for them because they cost $7.15 for 20 plasters. So she
went without.

The challenges of treating public and private patients play out every day at Charité, established in 1710 as a quarantine hospital outside Berlin. It fell into decrepitude after 1949. When the Wall came down in 1989, it had to merge with the richly endowed West German hospital system. "The East German system was bankrupt," says professor Karl Max Einhäupl, the chairman of Charité's board. (There was one MRI machine in all of the DDR in 1985.) The government invested $150 million or so every year just in Charité between 1992 and 1995.

Today there are economic tribulations. Charité, a hospital of last resort, lost an estimated $82 million on revenue of $1.6 billion last year. The state, once willing to lavish money on medical care, has turned tightfisted, putting in doubt a project to replace the 27-year-old tower that houses operating theaters, an ER and various departments. Einhäupl, who has spent most of his career treating patients, says he now spends one-third of his day on cost cutting. On the hospital wards it's up to people like orthopedic chief Perka to make the tough calls. Perka says he knows if he accepts a patient with an infection who has been transferred from another hospital, his department could potentially lose $72,000—which means "you will lose one doctor."

Other difficult choices loom for the entire system. "The development of medical sciences is so fast," opines Professor Einhäupl, "that in a few years it will be impossible for everyone" to benefit. Will the latest advancements be available just to private patients or the wealthy? "At some point," he says, "we will be under pressure—like the U.K. and the U.S."

In Brazil, Health Care Is Universal but Not Necessarily High Quality

Jeb Blount

In the following viewpoint, Jeb Blount argues that although Brazil has made an admirable constitutional commitment to providing universal health care, the quality of care is severely lacking. Blount claims that Brazil spends a modest amount of money on health care, but there are problems with irresponsible spending in the large country. Furthermore, he contends that the health care quality is inconsistent, with public hospitals excelling at certain acute treatments but failing to provide quality care for more basic health problems. Blount is a senior correspondent for FX Latin America at Thomson Reuters in Rio de Janeiro, Brazil.

As you read, consider the following questions:

1. According to Blount, the health care spending per person in Brazil is what fraction of the spending in the United States?

2. What percentage of the money spent by Brazil's clinics and hospitals on retail drugs is wasted or destroyed by poor management regulation and supervision, according to Blount?

3. Blount claims that public hospitals in Brazil do what one thing very well?

Jeb Blount, "Health Care in Brazil on $300 a Year," *World Policy Journal*, vol. 27, no. 2, Summer 2010, pp. 23–28. Copyright © 2010 World Policy Institute. All rights reserved. Reproduced by permission of SAGE Publications.

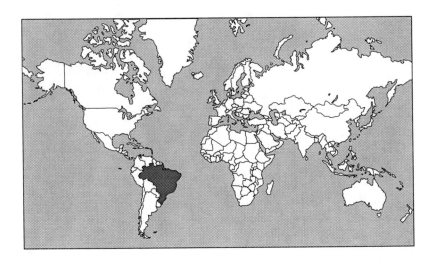

While new hospitals open throughout the country, the failure to provide the staff or the budget to maintain them has facilities falling into neglect just weeks after ribbons are cut. Thousands of Brazilians who have government—but not private—health coverage wait years for surgery. Doctors ditch their low-paying government jobs to see private patients, and don't show up for work at public clinics or hospitals. First-class emergency rooms and trauma centers are attached to underfunded, understaffed, dirty and disorganized hospitals. Universal drug programs for AIDS, hepatitis and tuberculosis exist alongside wasteful and destructive pharmacy subsidies. Through corruption and bad management, hundreds of millions of dollars in antibiotics and other important drugs are lost every year.

Health Care Spending in Brazil

In 2009, Brazil's government spent $367 per person on health care, according to the United Nations [UN] Development Programme. That's one-fourteenth as much as Luxembourg's government, the world's biggest per capita spender. It's less than one-eighth the $3,074 spent by the U.S. government. Brazil's federal government spends 3.6 percent of the nation's gross domestic product on health care, according to Sérgio Piola, a researcher at Ipea, Brazil's Institute of Applied Economic Research. That represents some $56 billion out of the $2.03 trillion GDP [gross domestic product] that Brazil, the world's eighth-largest economy, generated last year [2009]. According to Piola, Brazil must spend at least 6.5 percent of its GDP, or $132 billion a year, if it wants to fulfill its goal of a functioning universal health care system.

Even compared to the rest of Latin America, Brazil's government is well down the list of health spenders. Neighboring Argentina allocates more than twice as much—some $758 per capita annually—while Cuba spends $329 and Mexico $327. All three countries have better health care ratings and higher UN social-development rankings than Brazil. In the private sector, when private health care outlays are added, Brazil's spending leaps to 8.4 percent of gross domestic product—about $855 per person. In other words, this developing economy spends almost the same percentage of its national income on health care as the developed countries that form the OECD [Organisation for Economic Co-operation and Development], where spending is about 9 percent of GDP.

What does Brazil get for its money? Free health care—in theory. The 1988 constitution stipulates that health care for all is a fundamental right, and for nearly two decades, Brazil has provided many essential drugs to all who need them at no charge. Brazil's power as a single national buyer helps cut costs during negotiations with drug companies. Programs to provide free or subsidized drugs to the poor through public health clinics—"people's pharmacies"—or as part of special programs in privately owned drugstores have been expanded by federal, state and local governments in recent years. Packaging laws and awareness campaigns promote access to low-cost generics, and the generic drug companies take out ads on prime-time TV. Corinthians, Brazil's second-most popular soccer club, is financed by a generic drug company. When

Brazil is unable to get a good price for essential medicine, it overrides drug patents, buying or legalizing the purchase of copies from regulated generic drug producers around the world.

> Even compared to the rest of Latin America, Brazil's government is well down the list of health spenders.

Public health programs such as free condom distribution, neonatal counseling and triage in poor communities are reducing infant mortality and the spread of HIV. Vaccination for diseases such as measles and polio is mandatory and free. Public support for these programs is unanimous. "Nobody here thinks that it's wrong to have the government involved in health care," says Alexandre Barros, a top Brasília-based political risk consultant.

The results have also been dramatic. Life expectancy at birth has jumped 10 percent, while infant mortality has fallen by 59 percent. Still, making health care a free and universal right has hardly created a system where everyone receives quality care. Despite its merits, too often the system is inefficient or simply broken. . . .

Health care in Brazil claims to be universal, but good health care is not.

The Problem of Irresponsible Spending

In a country as large as Brazil—larger than the continental United States, a third of it blanketed by the Amazon jungle and river basin—the federal government has had difficulty providing care to all, or even figuring out where care is needed. Poor communities often lack basic health clinics that can provide access to immunizations, neonatal care and preventative medicine. A national bureaucracy isn't as agile as local representatives. When money was scarce, Brazil's health care failings weren't a major strain on the nation's budget or expectations. Now, these expectations have risen substantially, along with national wealth. No longer is $300 per person per year adequate. The political system is out of step with the nation's needs and desires.

Marcos is a doctor in northeastern Brazil. Two years ago, after working in public and private health clinics in a poor region outside Salvador, Brazil's third-largest city, he jumped at the chance to effect what he thought could be some real change. He accepted an appointment as secretary of health in a municipal government.

Marcos, who asked that his full name not be used, planned to purchase equipment for faster and more accurate diagnoses, saving money through preventive education. With the extra funds, he could create programs and facilities for some of the region's most serious problems, such as high blood pressure and diabetes. He was told he would be given a federal ATM card to pay for his approved programs. But once he received the card, he realized that the mayor was the only one with the access code, and he refused to pass it along to Marcos. Every request for funds involved discussions about who would receive contracts to supply goods and services for the programs. Requests for funds for the city's clinics were mostly rebuffed, and eventually Marcos turned the card over to the mayor. "In the end, I was not allowed to do anything," said Marcos. "I had responsibility, but no authority. It was the worst six months of my life. I quit."

Health care in Brazil claims to be universal, but good health care is not.

The problem was not a lack of funds, Marcos explained. Money was being spent, but was being wasted or diverted. Decisions were made based almost entirely upon the division of spoils from the federal government and the repayment of political debts. The health program came second. "We were getting great supplies in large quantity, the best available," Marcos said. "But instead of using them wisely, or buying something cheaper that would do just as well, the doctors would waste valuable resources. They'd use twice as much suture thread as they needed or give out unnecessary medicine."

While Marcos's case isn't an isolated incident, it's not indicative of local health programs either. The problem is deeper than that, and its roots can be traced to irresponsible spending. For example, Brazil has large funds set up to build sewage and water systems. While most Brazilians now have clean water, few cities have sewage treatment. Waterborne diseases still account for nearly a quarter of all illness in Brazil. Years of reliance on antibiotics have reduced interest in what was once a key part of health care planning: building waste treatment systems, properly storing food and mobilizing agencies to fight diseases like malaria, leprosy, dengue fever, Chagas' disease and cholera. While Brazil led the world in public health programs against AIDS, dengue fever returned, more than doubling to 585,000 cases in 2008 from 230,000 in 2000. Stopping dengue means wiping out mosquito breeding grounds in cities and addressing the lack of responsible water treatment head-on. It means house-to-house visits.

Problems with Health Care Quality

"Ignorance is probably our greatest problem," Marcos said. "Lots of people come to the clinic with the flu and feel cheated if they don't get some sort of medicine. They need to go home, drink fluids, take aspirin or Tylenol and sleep. But you need to put on a show or they don't take you seriously. Many of my patients don't have any idea about their bodies, about basic simple science. People want treatments, actions, facilities, when much cheaper things might do." But such ignorance does not end with the patients. For every serious cold or infection in Brazil, doctors immediately prescribe antibiotics. About 20 percent of the money spent by the country's clinics

Brazil's Health for All

The vision of a system providing "health for all" emerged [in Brazil] towards the end of the military dictatorship that started in 1964 and during the years of political opposition that was to a large extent framed in terms of access to health care. This struggle culminated in the 1988 constitution, which enshrined health as a citizens' right and which requires the state to provide universal and equal access to health services.

"Flawed but Fair: Brazil's Health System Reaches Out to the Poor," Bulletin of the World Health Organization, *April 2008.*

and hospitals on retail drugs is wasted or destroyed by poor management regulation and supervision, according to Brazil's federal pharmacy council. That's 1 billion reais ($570 million) that could go to better health care.

A block from my house sits the Hospital da Lagoa—a partly empty and decaying 10-story building. Designed by Oscar Niemeyer, one of the architects who designed the UN headquarters in New York, the building was a stunning modern structure when it opened in 1959. Once one of the best hospitals in Brazil, today it's a shadow of its former self. In 2000, Almir Munioz went to the Hospital da Lagoa, seeking medical care. A diabetic, his disease eventually progressed to the point where he needed to have his foot amputated. Wheeled from the operating room to the recovery area after surgery, he began hemorrhaging. He bled to death without anyone noticing. He lived across the street from the hospital with his wife and infant daughter. They were my neighbors.

Nearly 46 million Brazilians—almost a quarter of the population—have private health insurance. A case like Almir's is the reason. Even public servants and employees of state-owned companies get supplemental insurance, paid for by the government. The very people who administer Brazil's public systems don't trust the system themselves. This parallel system, too, is running into problems. In April, the special government secretariat that regulates the private system estimated that 11 percent of those paying for such insurance are receiving substandard benefits. My wife, my daughter and I pay about $600 a month for our private coverage—double the amount Brazil's federal government pays per person each year for its free public systems.

An Imbalanced System

The failures of the supposedly universal public system drive people into the private system, so taxpayers pay twice for their care: once when they pay income and sales taxes and again when they buy insurance. This is the classic bipolar imbalance of the Brazilian system. While there are some limited income tax write-offs for private insurance or medical bills, this only reduces the potential revenue available for the public system. And because large parts of Brazil's poor and lower middle class are exempt from income tax, they can't write off their private health costs. While they don't pay income tax, even poor Brazilians are still paying twice. Nobody is exempt from sales tax.

Nearly a third of all those who live in Brazil's rich southeast, where Rio de Janeiro and São Paulo are located, have private plans. They're designed to make sure that if they ever have to go to Hospital da Lagoa, the public hospital where my friend Almir died, they will have supplementary care. This public hospital, less than two blocks from the homes of two of Brazil's top politicians, has enough money for armed security guards, supplied by a company that has won large contracts to protect a wide range of government facilities. Though only a block from my house, public and free, I've never set foot in-side Hospital da Lagoa. Since I moved to the neighborhood in 1998, the hospital has closed its emergency room. In the 12 years I've lived in my neighborhood, I've never seen or heard anyone stand up for the hospital or seek to have it improved, and I live in a place where everyone gets quite worked up about bus noise or late-night Samba parties.

The very people who administer Brazil's public systems don't trust the system themselves.

Public hospitals in Brazil do one thing very well—trauma care. The government has also expanded paramedic ambulance services in major cities, which has allowed it to buy thousands of Brazilian-built ambulances from its auto industry, the country's largest sector, and emblazon them with the federal government's logos. If you are shot in Rio, which is one of the world's most violent cities—2,155 people were murdered here in 2009—pray you're taken to a public hospital. Hospitals can treat dozens of gunshot wounds a night. In addition to experienced cardio-thoracic surgeons, Brazil has developed specialties in orthopedic surgery, which stems the loss of limbs from bullets. If you end up in a public hospital and you haven't been shot, it is quite often another story.

Denis Wright had a car accident in Rio in April. Unconscious and suffering from burns, he was pulled from the wreck by firefighters and paramedics. As he came to, he was given a neck brace, carefully placed on a backboard and loaded into a modern ambulance filled with intensive care equipment. When he got to Miguel Couto Hospital, home to some of the world's finest trauma surgeons, it became a nightmare. He was transferred to a folding, wheeled stretcher for transport to the emergency facility. Within seconds the cart collapsed on itself and he tumbled onto another patient waiting on a mattress in a hallway packed with victims of car accidents, stabbings and other tragedies from a Saturday night in Rio. Orderlies re-extended the cart and put him back on it, only to have it collapse again. This time, he injured his head on the floor. Bruised from the fall, he was once more hoisted onto a new cart and sent on his way to the triage area, but the orderlies rounded a corner so quickly that the cart tipped over. By that time a friend had arrived. Despite his aching head and burns on his body, Wright got up, walked out and visited a doctor the next day.

Brazil is succeeding in many areas, but it's a long way from providing the comprehensive, universal care its constitution promises. It may do well to scale back its goals and focus on what it does well—serving the poor first, until it has the money and skills to reach more ambitious ends. It needs to take a less comprehensive and more realistic view of what its constitutional health rights entail. Brazil can write all it wants into a constitution (and, indeed, the 1988 document includes a whole potpourri—from the right to "sports justice" courts for athletes to permanent federal railway police) but if it can't even manage or pay for universal health care, disappointment will be inevitable and long lasting.

Periodical and Internet Sources Bibliography

The following articles have been selected to supplement the diverse views presented in this chapter.

Sharon Begley	"The Myth of 'Best in the World,'" *Newsweek*, March 22, 2008.
Mark B. Constantian	"Where U.S. Health Care Ranks Number One," *Wall Street Journal*, January 7, 2010.
Henry Featherstone	"Who Has the World's Best Healthcare System: The US or the UK? Neither," *Spectator* (UK), August 14, 2009.
Eduardo J. Gómez	"Brazil's Public Option: What Obama Can Learn from Lula About Universal Health Care," *Foreign Policy*, September 2, 2009.
David R. Henderson	"Health Care Is Worse Here than Elsewhere? It Just Ain't So!," *Freeman*, March 2008.
Richard Knox	"Most Patients Happy with German Health Care," NPR.org, July 3, 2008. www.npr.org.
Carrie L. Lukas	"National Health Care in Canada: Lessons in Rationing," Independent Women's Forum, Policy Brief, no. 24, July 23, 2009. www.iwf.org.
June E. O'Neill and Dave M. O'Neill	"Health Status, Health Care, and Inequality: Canada vs. the US," *Forum for Health Economics & Policy*, 2008.
Glen Whitman	"WHO's Fooling Who? The World Health Organization's Problematic Ranking of Health Care Systems," *Cato Institute Briefing Paper*, no. 101, February 28, 2008.
Wan Yanhai	"The Madness of China's Mental Health System," *Foreign Policy*, January 26, 2011.

CHAPTER 3

| The Cost of Health Care

In Europe, Health Care Costs Are Rising Faster than Available Funding

Economist Intelligence Unit

In the following viewpoint, the Economist Intelligence Unit argues that the future economic demands on Europe's health care systems will not be met by the current method of raising public funds. The author asserts that an older population with more chronic disease and costly technological advances in medicine are driving up the costs of health care. The author contends that the historical ways of collecting money for health care, through employment taxes and insurance premiums, are no longer providing adequate resources. The Economist Intelligence Unit started out as the in-house research outlet for the Economist, *but it now delivers business intelligence and advice to companies, financial institutions, governments, and universities.*

As you read, consider the following questions:

1. According to the Economist Intelligence Unit, the proportion of Europeans aged sixty-five years and older will grow to what percentage by 2030?

2. The full cost of bringing new medicines to market rose by what factor between 1975 and 2006, according to the author?

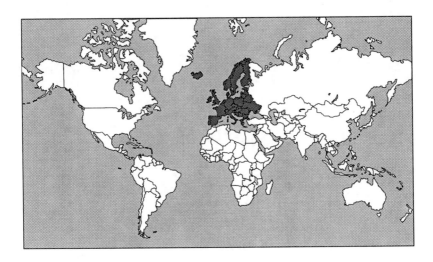

3. According to the Economist Intelligence Unit, when Europe's national health care systems were established in the 1930s and 1940s, the two main medical concerns were what?

Europe's ageing population provides both a testament to the success of healthcare provision in the past and a conundrum for the future. If healthcare had not made as many advances as it has, we would not be seeing the steady rise in life expectancy in all European countries, particularly the economically advanced ones. But success comes at a price: Older populations are succumbing to diseases which typically are more prevalent as longevity increases. These include a roster of chronic diseases, such as cancer, diabetes, heart disease, respiratory conditions, stroke, dementia, and depression. By definition, these chronic diseases do not kill quickly. That means the financial burden of caring for the chronically ill has grown heavier, as have the demands on the healthcare system to provide appropriate treatment and care.

Other factors are adding to the demands on the system. These include the spread of unhealthy lifestyles, the explosion in technology-based cures and the sophistication of the workforce required to administer those treatments, overly bureaucratic systems, increased specialisation in medicine, and the growing demand by an educated public for access to expensive modern medicine. The instruments used to raise public funds to pay for healthcare—taxation and insurance—cannot keep up with these stresses.

While higher life expectancy is good news, there is a downside: Older people are more likely to be prey to chronic disease.

Ageing and the Rise of Chronic Illness

In Europe the ratio of older to younger people is set to rise. The UN's [United Nations'] world population prospects report projects that the proportion of Europeans aged 65 years and older will grow from 16% in 2000 to 24% by 2030.

Life expectancy is also on the increase, particularly in the richer European countries. Eurostat figures show that life expectancy for male babies born in 2030 is more than a decade higher than that for those born in 1980 in the EU [European Union]-15 (generally the wealthier member states).

While higher life expectancy is good news, there is a downside: Older people are more likely to be prey to chronic disease, the product of deficiencies in genetic makeup that are innate and/or are triggered by long-term assault by unhealthy environments and lifestyles. When the level of "defective" genes reaches a critical level, one or more chronic diseases appear. A longer life span allows more time for this to occur. In 2010, over one-third of Europe's population is estimated to have developed at least one chronic disease.

So, while Europeans will live longer, they will not necessarily enjoy good health into old age.... Healthy life expectancy is between seven and ten years lower than average life expectancy.

The increasing likelihood of developing chronic disease later in life translates into higher healthcare costs. If poorly managed, chronic diseases can currently account for as much as 70% of health expenditures, partly because of the significant costs involved in hiring a workforce to care for sick older people. The costs to government could be higher still, were it not for the millions of people who voluntarily care for their loved ones. The EC [European Commission]-backed initiative, EQUAL, estimates the number of carers in the UK [United Kingdom], Italy and the Netherlands to be in the millions. Exacerbating the problem is the fact that the burden of paying for care will fall on a shrinking cohort of younger people.

The Cost of Technological Advances

The pace of innovation in material sciences, genetics, biotechnology, bioinformatics and e-health has escalated in recent years, bringing significantly improved chances of surviving disease. The impact on society is expected to be profound—as profound as the information technology (IT) revolution has been in transforming lives. Professor Hans-Georg Eichler, senior medical officer at the European Medicines Agency (EMA), is among those who expect to see major scientific breakthroughs in medicine. "My hope is that science will produce game changers," he says. "A game changer would be a drug that cures cancer, or a drug that stays the progression of dementia. These types of products are on the horizon." Yet few can predict when this next stage of medical evolution will occur.

Desirable though it is, this scientific endeavour is costly. Medical expenditure has skyrocketed as pharmaceutical, medical device and biotechnology companies have striven to develop new technologies and treatments, as well as meet high regulatory health and safety standards. Research and development (R&D) expenditure by pharmaceutical companies has grown rapidly over the past two decades. The full cost of

Healthy Life Expectancy Compared to Overall Life Expectancy

(Male Life Expectancy at birth (LE) and Healthy Life Expectancy (HALE) in Europe: developed versus developing countries. Last available data 2006-2008)

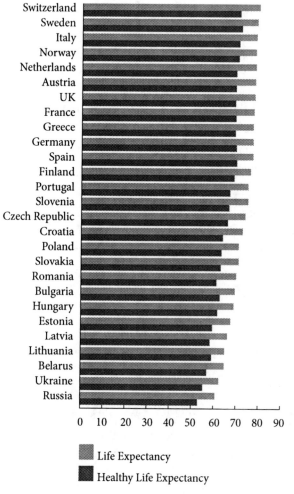

Source: *British Medical Journal.*

TAKEN FROM: Economist Intelligence Unit, "The Future of Healthcare in Europe," 2011. www.eufutureofhealthcare.com.

bringing new medicines to market rose tenfold between 1975 and 2006, when it reached over US$1.3bn [billion].

The skyrocketing costs, in turn, have led to further regulatory hurdles governing how much health authorities and individuals may spend on new medical technologies and medicines. For example, in May 2010 recession-hit Greece announced that it would cut drug prices by over 20%. Some manufacturers withdrew from the market, making certain medicines that were available elsewhere in Europe unavailable in Greece. Such inequities occur within countries as well. As Richard Bergström, director general of the Swedish Association of the Pharmaceutical Industry, explains, "The challenge we face is that there is already a lot of [financial] tension within healthcare systems, which has led to a blockade on access to medicines."

Patients are increasingly a major cost driver of healthcare systems.

While the financial pressures are real, an indiscriminate clampdown on spending could have far-reaching health consequences. Martin Bobrow, chairman of the Muscular Dystrophy Campaign in the UK, explains: "Policy makers need to be reminding themselves that biomedical research is in an explosive phase, and won't deliver goods if reined in thoughtlessly."

Patients are increasingly a major cost driver of healthcare systems. This occurs in two ways. First, access to online information about every aspect of health makes individuals more savvy healthcare consumers and more inclined to demand the latest (and likely expensive) medical innovations. Patients make these demands because they suspect that cash-strapped healthcare systems are unreasonably denying them the medical care they need.

Secondly, the spread of unhealthy lifestyles is driving up medical costs. For example, a high-calorie, fast-food culture has fed an epidemic of obesity, which in turn provides fertile ground for other diseases, such as type 2 diabetes, to develop. A 2007 government study in the UK, where levels of obesity are already among the highest in Europe, predicted an increase in excess of 60% in obesity-related diseases between 2005 and 2030.

Legacy Healthcare Structures

Among the biggest drivers of healthcare costs are the priorities that have governed the systems since their inception, and which are proving resistant to change. When Europe's national healthcare systems were established in the 1930s and 1940s, the two main medical concerns were the spread of infection and malnutrition. Today, with refrigerators, antibiotics and nutritious food generally available, these concerns are no longer paramount. Europeans are better nourished and less likely to contract communicable diseases. Now they are facing more intractable medical conditions: cancer, dementia, diabetes, heart disease, mental health problems and respiratory ailments, to name but a few.

As a population ages, the proportion of younger tax- or insurance-paying earners declines.

Yet little has changed since the 1950s in the way healthcare systems are run and how they are financed. Both the financing and delivery of healthcare remain highly fragmented and oriented to providing acute, rather than chronic, care. So, for example, many local communities retain their own full-service hospitals, resulting in system-wide duplication.

Mark Pearson, head of the health division at the OECD [Organisation for Economic Co-operation and Development], thinks the current situation in healthcare is archaic. "Healthcare systems in Europe look like they are designed for the 1950s. They are oriented around acute care. Medical education is oriented around hospitals. Payment systems are oriented around particular interventions," he says. "Biomedical research is still based on the assumption that people have single diseases at a time, but already the biggest challenge is multiple morbidities. These require a more longitudinal approach and payment systems that can cope with care provided in more than one setting. Success will mean finding some way to move on from the acute care model."

Moreover, despite increased average longevity, governments continue to finance their healthcare systems either out of tax revenue or out of insurance premiums, both of which depend on drawing money from a robust, healthy, relatively youthful workforce. As a population ages, the proportion of younger tax- or insurance-paying earners declines.

As a result of these legacy structures, healthcare consumes a growing proportion of GDP [gross domestic product] in developed countries.

Healthcare represented 9% of GDP for all OECD countries on average in 2008, with many Western European countries recording expenditure above that average.

Australia Should Emulate Singapore to Control Rising Health Care Costs

Richard Harper

In the following viewpoint, Richard Harper argues that Australia should implement health savings accounts, similar to those in Singapore, to control health care costs. Harper contends that the costs of health care in Australia are higher than they need to be because of a lack of competitive factors in Australia's publicly funded universal health care system. Allowing Australians to have health savings accounts that they can use at either public or private hospitals would reduce costs by increasing competition and individual prudence, Harper concludes. Harper is emeritus director of cardiology at the Monash Medical Centre, adjunct professor of medicine at Monash University, and holds a consultative position with the Department of Health for Victoria, Australia.

As you read, consider the following questions:

1. According to Harper, Singapore spends less than what percentage of its gross domestic product (GDP) on health?
2. The author proposes changing the Australian Medicare system to what kind of system?

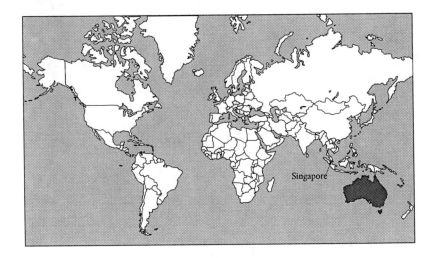

3. Harper claims that health savings systems encourage and reward what kind of behavior?

Few would argue against the need to change the cumbersome arrangements for funding and governance of Australia's hospitals. Unfortunately, the changes proposed by [Australian] Prime Minister Kevin Rudd do not address the main challenge to our health system—the need to constrain the ever-rising health costs of an ageing population.

Without such constraint, the principle of universal high-quality healthcare, which is the cornerstone of Medicare [in Australia], will eventually be unaffordable.

The Singapore Health System

In general, costs are high because health expenditure, whether private or public, is not subject to the usual competitive factors that govern ordinary commercial transactions. Two ways greater competition could be introduced into our health system without compromising care would be to change Medicare to a health-savings-based system and to allow public and private hospitals to compete for patients irrespective of their insurance status.

Singapore's Successful Health Care Model

Singapore's system has emerged as an impressive model. . . .

What's the reason for Singapore's success? It's not government spending. The state, using taxes, funds only about one-fourth of Singapore's total health costs. Individuals and their employers pay for the rest. In fact, the latest figures show that Singapore's government spends only $381 per capita on health—or one-seventh what the U.S. government spends. . . .

The reason the system works so well is that it puts decisions in the hands of patients and doctors rather than of government bureaucrats and insurers. The state's role is to provide a safety net for the few people unable to save enough to pay their way, to subsidize public hospitals, and to fund preventative health campaigns.

Rowan Callick, "The Singapore Model,"
American, May 27, 2008.

Singapore has such a system and spends less than 4 per cent of GDP [gross domestic product] on health—far less than Australia (9.7 per cent) and the US (15.4 per cent).

The difference is staggering yet the health outcomes and life expectancies are similar in all three countries. Indeed, in the most recent World Health Organization rankings, Singapore was rated sixth best in the world compared to Australia (32nd) and the US (37th).

The Singapore system is a compulsory savings scheme (Medisave) to which employees and employers contribute equally between 6 and 8 per cent of income, depending on age. Funds from Medisave can only be used to meet medical expenses, but citizens are unable to run up negative account balances and must pay additional expenses themselves or through voluntary health insurance (MediShield).

In general, costs are high because health expenditure, whether private or public, is not subject to the usual competitive factors that govern ordinary commercial transactions.

Citizens' accounts can also be used to pay expenses of immediate family members. The poor and needy, who may have a limited Medisave account and no health insurance, can apply to the government-appointed hospital Medifund committee for assistance in paying medical expenses.

Singapore does not provide the same degree of coverage as Medicare and disadvantages the poor, the unemployed and those with chronic illnesses. As such it is unlikely to be acceptable to the Australian public.

A Proposal for Australia

Our Medicare system could, however, be changed to a predominantly government-funded health savings account system offering the same safety net features of Medicare and without disadvantage to any group.

In this system, the federal government would pay a predetermined annual amount, indexed for age, into each citizen's health account held in a Commonwealth Health Bank. The account would be supplemented by an equal employer/employee contribution of 2 per cent of income. Funds from this account could only be used to pay for approved medical services at approved prices.

Hospital admissions, both public and private, would be paid for from the health savings accounts based on a case-mix system (the system by which Victorian public hospitals are currently funded and which Mr Rudd proposes nationwide).

Individual health practitioners and private hospitals could charge above the approved amounts, but the difference would need to be met from the individual's own pocket or private health insurance. Private insurance could also be used to cover catastrophic illnesses that would otherwise deplete health savings accounts.

There would be a safety net so that citizens could run up negative health balances (not allowed in Singapore) but for those earning income above a certain threshold, a marginally higher tax rate would apply until the balance was restored.

Health savings systems encourage and reward prudent behaviour without compromising health.

At death, a negative balance would have to be met from the deceased estate, a positive balance could be willed to another, and, during life, funds from a positive balance could be used to meet the medical expenses of another family member.

The Benefits of Competition

The safety net features of this scheme would mean that health expenditure would be significantly greater than Singapore's expenditure. Nevertheless, I believe substantial amounts would still be saved.

Health savings systems encourage and reward prudent behaviour without compromising health. A positive health account is an asset to be protected. It is a financial inducement to a healthy lifestyle and preventative medicine. With such a system, unnecessary visits to the doctor, over-ordering of tests and over-servicing (common in our system) would all be reduced. Competition between public and private hospitals for both insured and non-insured patients would result in further efficiencies and a reduction in waiting lists.

Let us not waste the opportunity for radical change in our health system. We must ensure we end up with the fairest and most cost-efficient system possible. Failure to achieve this will jeopardise our ability to provide universal healthcare for future generations.

Canada's Single-Payer System Controls Costs Better than America's System

Diane Francis

In the following viewpoint, Diane Francis argues that Canada's health care system has five major advantages over the US health care system. Francis claims that doctors' fees are cheaper in Canada, hospitals do not make profits, and drugs are cheaper. Francis contends that administrative costs of the system are also lower in Canada, as the US system has more complicated administration, marketing costs, and other expenses due to the extensive number of private health insurance plans. Francis concludes that Canada can benefit from the failure of the US health care system by selling services and drugs to Americans at lower costs. Francis is a columnist and editor at the National Post, *a Canadian newspaper in Toronto.*

As you read, consider the following questions:

1. According to Francis, which US president came up with the health care system that was adopted by Canada but not by the United States?

2. Income for physicians in the United States is approximately how much greater than that of Canadian physicians, according to the author?

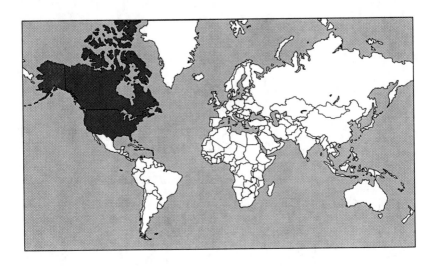

3. Francis claims that what four costs make American health care expenditures higher than those in Canada?

A s the health care establishment appears to be once again able to block any reasonable changes to America's sick health care system, it's important to note that ironically, the "father" of Canada's universal, single-payer health care system was the late president Lyndon B. Johnson [LBJ]. In 1964, his plan caused Canadian Prime Minister Lester Pearson to rush the same health care scheme into existence so that Ottawa was not beaten by the Americans, as was the case in 1934 with Social Security. As things turned out, LBJ compromised with the Republicans and scaled back his plan to a co-payer insurance for senior citizens, or Medicare.

So it's hardly surprising that, again, a popular president [Barack Obama] cannot win out against the nasty tactics and enormous wealth of the medical vested interests.

And yet, today Canada's system is not only as good as America's, but better medically according to the World Health Organization. Even more dramatic, it is between 30 and 60% cheaper for procedures, medications and hospital stays. Despite compelling evidence, the status quo remains south of the border and American voters/media appear to be unaware of the need for change. There are billions in profits being made at the expense of Americans and the country's economy.

The Canadian Advantage

1. Doctors' fees. According to health data collected by the Organisation for Economic Co-operation and Development [OECD], average income for physicians in the United States in 1996 was nearly twice that for physicians in Canada. (Doctors in Canada are self-employed, bill provinces for fees and are not employees of the governments.)

2. Hospitals are not-for-profit entities in Canada run on behalf of patients and governed by regional health boards which include physicians and other health professionals.

Today Canada's system is not only as good as America's, but better medically according to the World Health Organization.

---

3. Drugs are cheaper in Canada. In the U.S., US$728 per capita is spent each year on drugs, while in Canada it is $509. Patented drug prices in Canada are between 35% and 45% lower than in the United States, according to the OECD. (The price differential for brand-name drugs between the two countries has led Americans to purchase upward of US$1 billion in drugs per year from Canadian pharmacies.) This is because Canadian provinces buy drugs through a centralized system and get volume discounts. U.S. laws prohibit Medicare and Medicaid from doing so. The Canadian Patented Medicine Prices Review Board also can set a fair and reasonable price on patented products, based on comparisons with similar drugs and prices in similar countries. (Both countries are net importers of medications and industries in both spend 0.1% on research each year.)

Costs Under the Single-Payer System

Canada's is a single-payer, rather than a socialized, system. That means the government is the primary purchaser of services, but the providers themselves are private. (In a socialized system, the physicians, nurses, and so forth are employed by the government.) The virtue of both the single-payer and the socialized systems, as compared with a largely private system, is that the government can wield its market share to bargain down prices. . . .

A particularly high-profile example of how this works is Canadian drug reimportation. The drugs being bought in Canada and smuggled over the border by hordes of law-breaking American seniors are the very same pharmaceuticals, made in the very same factories, that we buy domestically. The Canadian provinces, however, bargain down the prices (Medicare is barred from doing the same). . . .

Single-payer systems are also better at holding down administrative costs. . . . This is largely because the Canadian system doesn't have to employ insurance salespeople, or billing specialists in every doctor's office, or underwriters. Physicians don't have to negotiate different prices with dozens of insurance plans or fight with insurers for payment. Instead, they simply bill the government and are reimbursed.

Ezra Klein, "The Health of Nations:
How Europe, Canada, and Our Own VA Do Health Care Better,"
American Prospect, *May 7, 2007.*

---

4. Administrative costs are dramatically lower in Canada than in the U.S. Administrative costs in the U.S. are double Canada's (according to a study in the *New England Journal of Medicine* 2003) plus healthcare providers and insurance companies have huge marketing costs. Here's the study done by the Department of Medicine, Cambridge Hospital and Harvard Medical School, Cambridge, Mass, USA:

"In 1999, health administration costs totaled at least US$294.3 billion in the United States, or US$1,059 per capita, as compared with US$307 per capita in Canada. After exclusions, administration accounted for 31.0 percent of health care expenditures in the United States and 16.7 percent of health care expenditures in Canada. Canada's national health insurance program had overhead of 1.3 percent; the overhead among Canada's private insurers was higher than that in the United States (13.2 percent vs. 11.7 percent). Providers' administrative costs were far lower in Canada. Between 1969 and 1999, the share of the U.S. health care labor force accounted for by administrative workers grew from 18.2 percent to 27.3 percent. In Canada, it grew from 16.0 percent in 1971 to 19.1 percent in 1996. (Both nations' figures exclude insurance-industry personnel.) CONCLUSIONS: The gap between U.S. and Canadian spending on health care administration has grown to 752 dollars per capita. A large sum might be saved in the United States if administrative costs could be trimmed by implementing a Canadian-style health care system."

Today, and not surprisingly, a medical tourism business in Canada is growing rapidly as Americans go north to take advantage of lower costs.

---

5. *Other costs* also add to American health care expenditures dramatically: government administrative red tape, requirements for record-keeping, a diversity of accounts receivable insurers and a patchwork quilt of plans and layers of authority to deal with.

Higher payment for doctors has created a brain drain of physicians from Canada to the U.S., but in 2005 this reversed, according to the Canadian Institute for Health Information (CIHI).

Today, and not surprisingly, a medical tourism business in Canada is growing rapidly as Americans go north to take advantage of lower costs. Now that the Americans appear to have blown another chance to fix their health care system, it's time for Canadian physicians and others to ratchet up the industry, offering selective services to Americans.

Taiwan's Health Care System Delivers Quality with Low Costs

Ian Williams

In the following viewpoint, Ian Williams argues that Taiwan's single-payer health care system compares favorably in terms of cost and quality to the United States, United Kingdom, Canada, and other advanced nations. Williams contends that Taiwan's program of co-payments helps to keep costs down and to manage demand. He claims that Taiwan's national health insurance system pays for itself through revenue collection from a variety of sources, adjusting revenues to costs as needed. Williams argues that the government's monopoly power has worked well to control costs without abuse. Williams is a regular columnist for the Guardian, *a British daily newspaper.*

As you read, consider the following questions:

1. According to Williams, polls in 2005 showed what percentage satisfaction rate among the Taiwanese for their health insurance?

2. In 2005 Taiwan's National Health Insurance program introduced what system to contain costs, according to the author?

Ian Williams, "Health Care in Taiwan: Why Can't the United States Learn Some Lessons?," *Dissent*, vol. 55, no. 1, Winter 2008, pp. 13–17. Copyright © 2008 by the Foundation for the Study of Independent Social Ideas, Inc. All rights reserved. Reprinted with permission of the University of Pennsylvania Press.

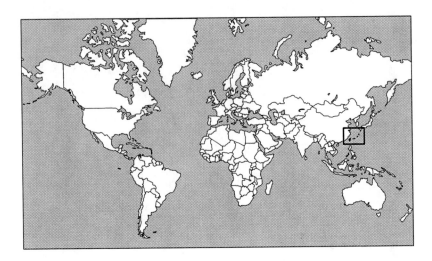

3. According to Williams, what percentage of the cost of
Taiwan's National Health Insurance program is borne by
the government, employers, and employees?

Taiwan inaugurated its National Health Insurance [NHI]
program in 1995. Before then the three major social health
insurance programs, labor insurance, government employee
insurance, and farmers' insurance, left 40 percent of the population uncovered, many of them children and retirees. Dr.
Michael Chen, vice president and chief financial officer of the
NHI Bureau, says that there is now 99 percent coverage—he is
not sure who the missing 1 percent are, but suspects that they
are expatriates who have not registered (apparently, prison in-
mates are not covered but do receive care in the prison
system). Indeed, many expatriates maintain their coverage—
including the million or so who now work in mainland China.
Conversely, foreign workers in Taiwan are also covered.

The Taiwanese Health Care System

NHI premiums cover Western- and Chinese-style medicine,
both in- and outpatient, prescription charges, home care, and
dentistry. Almost all Western-style hospitals and 88 percent of

Chinese-medicine clinics are in the system. Though dentists have been opting out of the British national health dental system in large numbers, almost 95 percent of dental clinics are in the Taiwanese system. Health care is provided by a competitive mixture of municipal and public (about one-third of the beds) and privately owned hospitals that also offer comprehensive primary care. Between them they employ almost two-thirds of doctors. Avoiding the severe conflict of interest that the British system has maintained, doctors contracted to hospitals cannot run private practices on the side.

Taiwan had a vigorous market-based health provision system, which has adapted itself, apparently very happily, to the new national service.

Taiwan is a smaller (twenty-one million people), more compact country than the United States, but the NHI provides many pointers for Americans attempting to secure full health coverage. To begin with, Taiwan had a vigorous market-based health provision system, which has adapted itself, apparently very happily, to the new national service. The former Kuomintang [KMT] government was an authoritarian social democracy, in the very limited sense that social provision was on the agenda. But corruption and capitalism were fully developed. The NHI was introduced in the early days of democracy, just as the KMT single-party system was being dismantled. It was a popular election issue.

The provision of health care is not nationalized, despite a degree of information and coordination that, for example, the British system cannot match after spending billions on computerization. Rather, the NHI is a classic single-payer scheme—the government runs a compulsory, mostly premium-financed insurance system, which negotiates a single payment schedule with the private and municipal or government-owned providers.

The Cost of Health Care

On the face of it, the experience of the insured in Taiwan is certainly better than that of Americans dependent on the caprices of commercial health insurers. In 2005, polls showed a 72.5 percent satisfaction rate—and much of the dissatisfaction is with the cost, laughably small though it is by U.S. standards. When co-payments and premiums were increased in 2002, the satisfaction rate plummeted to 59.7 percent. To put this in perspective, the premiums at the maximum are less than $20 (U.S.) per month (the annual per capita GDP [gross domestic product] is $16,500 U.S.).

In 2003, health spending per head in Taiwan was less than $800 per head of population compared to the U.S. level of approximately $5,500.

Taiwan has done this for proportionately, less than half the cost of the United States, with costs running at 6.2 percent of gross domestic product in 2005, compared with the following for other countries: United States, 15.2 percent; France, 10.1 percent; Canada, 9.9 percent; United Kingdom, 7.7 percent; Japan, 7.9 percent; South Korea, 5.2 percent (World Health Organization figures for 2003 published in 2006).

In absolute terms, the difference is even starker. In 2003, health spending per head in Taiwan was less than $800 per head of population compared to the U.S. level of approximately $5,500. In fact, by 2005, U.S. health care spending increased 6.9 percent to almost $2.0 trillion, or $6,697 per person, amounting to 16 percent of GDP.

With an aging population demanding more and more innovative medical interventions, the NHI faces similar problems to the United States in terms of the escalation of demand (and thus of cost), but it has contained the growth of health care costs as a share of GDP while expanding coverage to a far higher proportion of hitherto uninsured people than in the United States.

The various constituencies seem to have cooperated to avert long-term financial problems, adjusting premiums, co-payments, and provider fees in a way that has left them all reasonably content, while providing protection for weaker and poorer groups and those suffering chronic illnesses. Even the generous safety net seems to have another net below, with exemptions for those who cannot pay, loan option to pay premiums, and referral to charitable organizations for payment when even that fails. For example, by the end of 2004, the NHI had issued 750,000 "Catastrophic Illness" cards, whose holders' co-payments are either reduced or eliminated entirely. This makes sound social but bad financial sense, as these people account for almost a quarter of the bureau's expenditure—but that is what national insurance is about.

Taiwan's program of nominal co-payments, with suitable provision for the genuinely needy, seems a sensible way to manage and filter demand.

A common argument against "socialized medicine" in the United States is that it leads to rationing and waiting lists for treatment. However, unlike the Canadian or British systems, and, indeed, unlike health maintenance organizations in the United States, there are simply no waiting lists, except perhaps for organ donor availability. That is in part because, although there is a government sponsored single-payer system, there is not a single provider, and the insured have free choice of doctors and institutions. Indeed, Deputy Minister of Health Tsay Jinn Chen refers to "doctor shopping" on the part of the insured, which introduces market discipline and ensures speedy treatment.

Managing Costs and Demand

Of course, the system did not start running as designed immediately. It has needed adjustment, not least to balance revenue and costs and manage demand in a way that does not impinge on health care. In fact, the system does seem to have a considerable degree of adaptability.

When the British National Health Service was established in 1947, there were two major fiscal problems. One was that, as Health Minister Aneurin Bevan said, he had to "stuff the maws of doctors with gold" to get them into the system. That was in part because the government was, in effect, nationalizing the old hospitals and employing the doctors on a contractual basis. The other problem, which would be relevant for any U.S. introduction of national insurance, was the "overhang," the pent-up demand for dentistry, prescription medicine, dentures, and glasses from millions of previously uncovered patients. In Taiwan, Chen described the new system as something like "an all-you-can-eat" restaurant for very hungry people, who no longer had to trade off other purchases against health care.

The introduction of co-payments in Britain in the early 1950s, as a result of the costs of the Korean War, occasioned a huge ideological battle in the Labour Party, with Harold Wilson, later the prime minister, leading a revolt on behalf of a completely free service. In retrospect, admirable though the motives of the Labour revolt may have been, Taiwan's program of nominal co-payments, with suitable provision for the genuinely needy, seems a sensible way to manage and filter demand.

In order to contain costs, in 2005 the NHI introduced a referral system, aimed at dissuading the insured from racing to the most prestigious hospital or specialist with every headache. They can still do that, but now they face an increased co-payment if they skip referral. The co-payments should not dissuade anyone genuinely ill from seeking help—it is a mere

$12 U.S. for an un-referred patient who chooses to go to an academic medical center. For those who go first to a clinic, referred or un-referred, the co-payment is $1.50 U.S.

For some expensive high-tech and experimental procedures pre-authorization is needed, but it would appear that this is less onerous than dealing with an American HMO [health maintenance organization]. Equitably counterbalancing the co-payments are ceilings on in-treatment liabilities—for example, an annual cumulative ceiling of approximately $1,300 or 10 percent of per capita income for co-payments. The ceiling has a safety net hanging from it as well, with many exceptions for serious illness, childbirth, rural and outlying areas, and low-income families, to ensure that no one is deterred from seeking the help they need.

Prescription costs are managed similarly. First, the NHI bargains down drug prices, and second, co-payments are on a proportional scale with a ceiling of approximately $6. Once again, there are many exemptions for the needy.

A Card That Improves Quality

The NHI benefits from a long-standing public health system that, even under the Kuomintang, provided a network of inoculation and vaccination, children's and women's health care, and which had reduced or eliminated the diseases that otherwise would be prevalent in a subtropical developing country. The NHI is proud, for example, of its 95 percent inoculation rate against measles, which compares to 70 percent in Japan.

Although the competitive free market in health was probably an important factor in averting waiting lists, it did have other consequences, one of which, as Jui-Fen Rachel Lu and William C. Hsiao charge, is that "Taiwan has a fragmented health care delivery system that lacks continuity of care. Its clinical quality of care suffers from years of laissez-faire policy toward clinical practices." There are, however, more and more quality controls. By law, only licensed doctors can own a hospital or clinic, for example. Building on that, the persuasive power of the NHI has been creating a family doctor system, in which between five to ten primary care clinics in each area are networked with NHI contracted hospitals to provide an integrated care system, with referrals when needed but with primary care continuity.

One of the most valuable applications of the NHI's information system is that of tracking down suspected cases and heading off an epidemic disease.

It seems that the family practice is an innovation for Taiwan, but harnessed to the network, and with the detailed record keeping made possible by the NHI card, it ensures better primary care. A smart chip in the new insurance cards allows the NHI to look for examples of fraud, overbilling, and similar practices that bedevil [U.S.] Medicare. There are significant fringe benefits, too, for example, keeping track of organ donors, which is especially important in a society where donation is not that common.

NHI providers use the card for financial purposes but also increasingly for clinical record keeping. Since 2004, the IC [integrated circuit] card has given users access to details of serious illness and injury and major medical examinations and scans, avoiding unnecessary and expensive repeat tests of the kind that happen so frequently in the United States. It stores records of both prescriptions and drug allergies, thus averting the problems of adverse interactions between different medicines, and duplication of prescriptions for dangerous or expensive drugs. In previous years the system was prone to overprescribing and prescription inflation, but the card checked that tendency. One of the most valuable applications of the NHI's information system is that of tracking down suspected cases and heading off an epidemic disease, as in the case of SARS [severe acute respiratory syndrome].

The card makes it much easier to monitor and detect fraud. In 2004, the NHI reduced or deducted claims from over a thousand institutions, 231 were awarded demerits, which affect their contract payment levels, and 90 were suspended from the system for periods of one to three months. Four were dropped entirely. The information system is so effective that a former CEO [chief executive officer] of the NHI Bureau once quipped that he knew immediately if the same tooth had "been pulled twice" from any individual.

The Sources of Revenue

The IC card helps track payment of premiums and allows prompt reminders of missed premium payments, which ensures coverage for the insured and, equally vital, cash flow for the system. Since it was set up, the costs of the NHI have risen by an annual average of 5.5 percent, while revenues have only risen by 4.7 percent, hence the need for constant fine-tuning of co-payments and attempts to restrain expenditures, which are currently between $11 and $12 billion U.S. The fund is mandated to carry a one-month buffer but has rarely been able to do so. Solutions have included doubling the tobacco tax surcharge and raising the earnings ceiling on contributions, which currently stands at a little over $4,000 per month.

Premium collection is similar to that of Social Security contributions in the United States. Employers and the self-employed are legally bound to pay. However, unlike the U.S. Social Security fund, the NHI is a genuine pay-as-you-go system. The aim is for the premium income to pay costs.

There is a continual tussle over who bears the cost of the national service—currently 27 percent is paid by the government, 35 percent by employers, and 38 percent by employees. The various partners try to shift the burden, and legislators are reluctant to incur popular displeasure by increasing costs to employees, while the influential employers' organizations also have the ear of negotiators. They talked down the employers' share of the premium from 80 percent to 60 percent. The government puts in another 10 percent.

The government share, including the tobacco tax surcharge and lottery proceeds, goes disproportionately—but appropriately—to finance the premiums of disadvantaged groups, remote rural dwellers, the indigenous peoples, and the poor. Although all contributors have access to the same services, there is a significant redistributive effect. Six categories of insured pay at different levels, scaled against income, with ceilings.

The single-payer system means that the NHI is a monopoly purchaser and so has greater bargaining power with the pharmaceutical companies and with the providers.

The insured pay for each dependent, up to a ceiling of three, while the employers pay for an average number of dependents, which takes away the incentive to fire or not hire fecund workers. For the "regional population," in remote rural areas, the government pays 40 percent and the insured pays 60 percent of the premium, while for low-income households, the government pays the whole premium.

The Benefit of Monopoly Power

The single-payer system means that the NHI is a monopoly purchaser and so has greater bargaining power with the pharmaceutical companies and with the providers. As in Canada and the United Kingdom, the pharmaceutical companies have to accept reasonable prices, because the NHI has a weight in prescription pricing that is deliberately denied Medicare in the latest U.S. Medicare prescription plan.

Facing up to the pharmaceutical industry allows the single-payer system to control costs, and the technology of the NHI card allows controls of overcharging. It even encourages best practices, such as appropriate use of antibiotics for upper respiratory chest infections, or antacids for stomach problems. The twenty-nine million monthly claims going through the system allow effective analysis of costs and billing patterns.

The NHI does not seem to have abused its monopoly power to drive down doctors' earnings, as there is vigorous competition among practitioners and institutions for patient patronage, even at the fees collectively agreed upon. The ease of payment, with the government writing the checks, seems to have been a good enough trade-off for the doctors. There is nothing to stop a doctor setting up private practice—except a shortage of clients. The system was originally based on fee for service but then transitioned to a "case-payment" system based on fifty-three items. The program's chief financial officer, Michael Chen, says that the idea is that the NHI is purchasing "not just medical care, but health, as evidenced by initiatives aiming at encouraging 'pay for performance.'" The 95 percent inoculation rate against measles suggests the success of the program.

The NHI Committee for the Arbitration of Medical Costs considers not only the overall figures but also individual providers' performance based on support for patients' rights, accessibility and satisfaction, efficiency of service, and similar criteria. The committee rewards providers if scored for "excellence" through the "quality assurance funds." . . .

The Taiwanese system begins with an idealistic premise—of universal, high-quality health coverage—but then addresses in a most pragmatic way the actual behavior of the constituencies involved: the medical providers, the pharmaceutical companies, and the patients. The frequent readjustments do not pander to the moral panic of freeloading or fraud that often governs legislation and decision making in the United Kingdom and the United States, but rather to actual, observable behavior.

In Africa, Fees for Health Care Keep People from Seeking Treatment

Oxfam International

In the following viewpoint, Oxfam International argues that charging user fees is an unfair method of paying for health care. Oxfam contends that evidence from Africa shows that even small user fees keep poor people from accessing basic health care. Oxfam claims that if user fees are removed, utilization of health services increases, benefitting the poor. The organization cautions that increased spending is necessary to offset the removal of fees and that efforts need to be made to ensure that health care expansion occurs. Oxfam International is a confederation of fifteen organizations working together to find lasting solutions to poverty and injustice.

As you read, consider the following questions:

1. According to Oxfam International, what charge for bed nets in Kenya reduced demand by 75 percent?

2. According to the author, when Uganda removed all health user fees at public facilities, attendance at the clinics increased by what percentage?

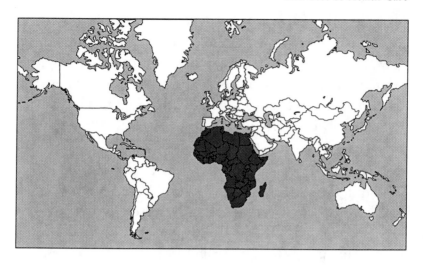

3. Oxfam International advocates for increasing spending on health to at least what percentage of national spending?

Uer fees are the most inequitable way of paying for health care. User fees are a key factor in preventing poor people from accessing the health care they need and evidence suggests they lead to higher infant and maternal mortality rates. Surveys conducted in Sierra Leone, Burundi, Mali, Democratic Republic of the Congo, Chad and Haiti all reveal a common pattern of exclusion of patients linked to payment for health care.

User Fees and Access to Care

In Rwanda, when health fees were introduced in 1996, take-up of health services halved. In one Nigerian district, the numbers of women dying in childbirth doubled after fees were introduced for maternity services, and the number of babies delivered in hospitals declined by half. Similar consequences of user fees have been observed in Tanzania and Zimbabwe.

Recent work in Africa has shown how even small payments associated with the social marketing of mosquito nets reduce uptake, and make such investments far less cost effective than free public distribution. Charging pregnant women only US$0.75 for an insecticide-treated bed net in Kenya for example reduced demand by 75%. In the same country, a small charge introduced for deworming drugs reduced uptake of this highly cost-effective treatment by 80%.

In Ethiopia fees charged by public health clinics are a primary reason why people opt for self-care. In Sudan 70% of people in disadvantaged areas who did not seek care when sick reported scarcity of money as the reason for not accessing services. Making households pay for health care excludes women and girls, who are usually last in line for services.

User fees are a key factor in preventing poor people from accessing the health care they need.

Attempts to target poor people and exempt them from paying fees have failed. In Zambia only 1% of exemptions were granted on the basis of poverty, indicating that either poor people were staying away or being forced to pay.

Now the world faces an unprecedented economic crisis, the full impact of which is still to be felt in poor countries. Lessons from previous crises show that as household incomes decline more people switch from fee-paying private services to seek free services in the public sector. When free services are unavailable in the public sector the number of people denied health care increases dramatically.

Abolishing health care fees for all and supporting essential health care for mothers and young children would not cost much—in relative terms less than £1 billion [British pounds] a year. That's just £1.38 per person in sub-Saharan Africa. For such a small amount there can surely be no justification for governments and aid donors leaving fees in place, blocking access to health care and impoverishing millions of people.

The Benefits of Removing Fees

User fees were introduced in many poor countries in the 1980s and 1990s, often as a condition of lending from the World Bank and IMF [International Monetary Fund]. The evidence is now very clear that, as the director general of the World Health Organization recently stated, 'user fees have punished the poor'. In recognition of this, a number of developing countries are leading the way in removing fees. Their experiences show that abolishing fees can have an immediate impact on the uptake of health services when supported by policies to address increased utilisation and loss of revenue.

In Uganda, in the run up to the election in 2001, the president removed all health user fees in public facilities. Service use increased suddenly and dramatically with an 84% increase in attendance at clinics countrywide. Research by the World Bank found the increase in service use was highest for the poorest income groups showing that free health care in Uganda is pro-poor. Importantly, the gains made in Uganda have been sustained. This has been helped by investment in expanding health care delivery and the implementation of quality improvement measures put in place following problems of drug stock-outs in facilities.

Abolishing fees can have an immediate impact on the uptake of health services when supported by policies to address increased utilisation and loss of revenue.

The trend to remove health fees in Africa has been gathering pace. In the past couple of years Zambia, Burundi, Niger, Liberia, Kenya, Senegal, Lesotho, Sudan, and Ghana have abolished fees for key primary health care services for at least some target population groups, most commonly children and pregnant women. The challenge remains to fully implement these policies and extend free care to all. Nevertheless, initial evidence shows promising results.

In Niger, after fees were removed for children and pregnant women in 2006, consultations for under fives quadrupled and antenatal care visits doubled. In Burundi, average monthly births in hospitals rose by 61% and the number of caesarean sections went up by 80% following the abolition of fees for maternity services. When fees were removed in rural areas in Zambia, utilisation rates of government facilities increased by 50%. Districts with a greater proportion of poor people recorded the greatest increase in utilisation. Furthermore, while Zambia continues to face severe health worker shortages patients themselves report no deterioration in the quality of care since user fees were removed.

In Asia too, a UK [United Kingdom] government-funded study comparing health systems across the continent found that in low-income countries, the most pro-poor health systems were those providing universal coverage of health services that were free or almost free.

The Removal of User Fees

Announcements of free health care are not enough to ensure a sustainable increase in access to health care. Any announcements must therefore be accompanied by a broader package of supportive action to ensure that free services are actually available to and used by poor people and that official fees are not merely replaced by informal fees. Countries not immediately able to implement free health care for the entire population could phase it in by initially providing free services for women and children.

Developing countries wishing to remove user fees now, or to improve and extend existing free health care, can benefit from experiences of other countries and from tool kits developed by experienced agencies.

In every successful case, strong and high-level political leadership and commitment to free health care has preceded the removal of user fees. The evidence is also clear that in any country health spending must increase to offset lost revenue and pay for the increased demand resulting from user fee removal. Failure to increase spending could lead to falling quality of care generated by drug shortages and staff difficulties in managing increased workloads.

Additional financing for health workers and drugs can be mobilised at the domestic level by increasing spending on health to at least 15% of national spending (as promised in the 2001 Abuja Declaration), through improvements in tax revenue collection systems and more equitable distribution of existing resources. Such action at the national level is essential but on its own cannot raise the level of resources required to achieve health care for all. It must therefore be complemented by additional long-term and predictable financing from rich country governments and multilateral aid agencies, delivered using government budgets and plans. Additional resources for free care should be mobilised through aid, debt relief, innovative financing and measures such as tackling tax havens and tax evasion.

The challenges to quality and supply of health care arising from removing fees are real but are certainly not insurmountable.

Secondly, free health care policies must be carefully planned and implemented so that health workers and the health system as a whole are fully prepared for the change. Effective communication to staff and the public are particularly essential to avoid confusion and to ensure citizens are fully aware of their rights under the new policy.

Thirdly, efforts should be made by all actors to link the removal of user fees to broader health system improvements to ensure an overall expansion in public health care coverage. This should include support from international donors for: appropriate and equitable health financing mechanisms; strategies to expand and retain the health workforce; improving and expanding drug supply; scaling up the number of health care facilities especially in rural areas; and tackling other significant barriers to access including the low status and lack of empowerment of women, transport costs, poor quality of care, women's education and general knowledge and understanding of health.

The challenges to quality and supply of health care arising from removing fees are real but are certainly not insurmountable. Sadly, these same challenges continue to be used by some senior ranking donor and developing country government officials as a reason to leave user fees in place. Such inaction will continue to deny access to health care for millions of people and is unacceptable in light of increasing evidence and understanding of how to make free health care a success.

Periodical and Internet Sources Bibliography

The following articles have been selected to supplement the diverse views presented in this chapter.

AVERT	"AIDS, Drug Prices and Generic Drugs," 2011. www.avert.org.
Rowan Callick	"The Singapore Model," *American*, May 27, 2008. www.american.com.
Arthur Garson Jr.	"Healthcare's Wasted Billions," *Christian Science Monitor*, October 8, 2008.
Regina E. Herzlinger	"Switzerland Has the Medical Bills Covered," *Times* (UK), January 27, 2009.
Toni Johnson	"Healthcare Costs and U.S. Competitiveness," Council on Foreign Relations, Backgrounder, March 23, 2010. www.cfr.org.
Niko Karvounis	"Health Care in Singapore," *Taking Note* (blog), July 31, 2008. http://takingnote.tcf.org.
Hala Kodmani	"Health Care in France on $3,000 a Year," *World Policy Journal*, Summer 2010.
Konstanty Radziwill	"What Are the Minimal Services to Be Provided by the Healthcare System?," *World Medical Journal*, October 2010.
T.R. Reid	"It's Just What the Doctor Ordered," *Newsweek*, August 16, 2010.
John Stossel	"There's No Such Thing as Free Health Care: The Costly Truth About Canada's Health Care System," *Reason*, July 2, 2009.
Ross Tieman	"Healthcare in France, Who Pays, and Who Supplies," *Financial Times*, April 30, 2009.

CHAPTER 4

Disease-Related Challenges for Health Care

Despite Some Progress, HIV Remains a Global Health Challenge

Joint United Nations Programme on HIV/AIDS (UNAIDS)

In the following viewpoint, the Joint United Nations Programme on HIV/AIDS (UNAIDS) argues that progress is being made in preventing and treating HIV and AIDS throughout the world, but there are areas where more can be done. UNAIDS contends that the AIDS epidemic has hit Africa the worst; though new infections have slowed and treatment has increased, the gains are fragile and dependent on new funding. UNAIDS contends that many regions of the world could do more to provide treatment, increase education, and remove social barriers to prevention. UNAIDS aims to lead and inspire the world in achieving universal access to HIV prevention, treatment, care, and support.

As you read, consider the following questions:

1. According to the Joint United Nations Programme on HIV/AIDS (UNAIDS), the HIV incidence rate declined by more than what percentage between 2001 and 2009?

2. According to the author, the bulk of 2009 spending on HIV and AIDS in Eastern Europe and Central Asia was in which country?

3. What percentage of the population in the Caribbean is infected with HIV, according to UNAIDS?

In graphics depicting the global AIDS epidemic there is always one piece of the pie chart that is biggest, one vertical column that is tallest, one trend line that is steepest: Africa. What has been happening in Africa over the past 30 years is the greatest public health challenge in human history.

AIDS in Africa

Yet some of the most progressive and demanding AIDS policies come out of Africa. The Abuja Declaration, the Maputo Plan of Action, the Kampala Heads of State Summit and, most recently, the African Union Health Ministers' Common Position, all aim to conquer AIDS.

Some 22.5 million people now live with HIV in Africa.

Coverage of services to prevent new child infections increased from 15% in 2005 to 54% in 2009. The HIV incidence rate declined by more than 25% between 2001 and 2009. Antiretroviral treatment coverage is increasing. Almost all governments on the continent have national AIDS plans, and some of the most heavily affected countries are projected to achieve universal access. Africa's Common Position acknowledges universal access across the continent may take longer than 2015, and urges governments to quickly integrate the AIDS response into "national development instruments" and pursue "evidence-informed and rights-based responses". It spurs the prevention revolution by committing to "halve the number of infections by 2015", mandating legal systems to "eradicate HIV-related stigma and discrimination", and challenging researchers to "accelerate vaccine and microbicide development".

Some 22.5 million people now live with HIV in Africa. The majority (60%) are women and girls. HIV prevalence is as high as 25% in some countries, and the rate of people becoming newly infected outpaces treatment access. Of the 16.6 million children globally who have lost one or both parents to an AIDS-related illness, 14.9 million are in Africa.

The Asia-Pacific region has made significant progress in controlling HIV's spread.

As international aid falters, many have called for African governments to contribute more of their own resources regardless of their national income. International organizations, donors and governments must resolve the contradiction between need and the capacity to pay if fragile progress is to be strengthened and global commitment to shared responsibility is to be renewed.

AIDS in the Asia-Pacific Region

The Asia-Pacific region has made significant progress in controlling HIV's spread. The number of people living with HIV has remained stable for the past five years and estimated new infections are 20% lower than in 2001. Thailand, Cambodia and certain parts of India have turned their epidemics around by providing quality services to their key populations at higher risk. Cambodia is one of eight countries worldwide to have reached universal access to antiretroviral therapy (94% coverage). Significantly fewer children are getting HIV and dying from AIDS than 10 years ago, and two countries report 80% coverage of services to prevent new child infections.

These gains, however, are insufficient and fragile. In 2009, median reported prevention coverage for people who inject drugs was 17%; for men who have sex with men 36.5%; and for female sex workers 41%. Programmes in key affected populations to prevent transmission to intimate sexual partners are severely lacking.

The region demonstrates that sustained access to HIV treatment must go hand in hand with sustained access to prevention for key populations at higher risk.

There are laws obstructing the rights of people living with HIV and those most vulnerable to HIV infection in 90% of the region, and 16 countries restrict their travel. Sex with a same-sex partner is criminalized in 20 countries, while 29 countries criminalize some aspect of sex work. Eight countries compulsorily detain people who use drugs and 11 apply the death penalty for drug offences. Distributing needles and syringes to drug users is prohibited in seven countries. Such punitive environments damage public health as the marginalized are unlikely to seek services.

According to the latest UNGASS [United Nations General Assembly Special Session] reports, AIDS expenditures in 2009 totalled US$1.07 billion. Estimates based on the methodology suggested by the Commission on AIDS in Asia indicate that US$3.3 billion is needed for a targeted response across the region. International funding accounted for more than 50% of AIDS spending in most of the region's countries. To reach universal access, a rapid increase in domestic funding is needed, particularly in middle-income countries, which would need to spend less than 0.5% of gross national income to fund their response.

The Asia Pacific Regional Consultation on Universal Access brought together more than 250 participants from 27 countries in Bangkok in March 2011. Governments, civil society, United Nations agencies and other development partners were represented.

Civil society and regional governmental bodies played leading roles in the debates, while young leaders from key affected populations demanded a voice in the HIV response.

The consultation delivered a thorough and progressive resolution that prescribed the following actions to achieve the targets of zero new HIV infections, zero discrimination and zero AIDS-related deaths: instigate a prevention revolution focusing on key populations at higher risk; increase efforts to sustain gains in treatment; and redress legal barriers, stigma and discrimination, and funding gaps.

AIDS in Eastern Europe and Central Asia

Seventeen countries in Eastern Europe and Central Asia (EECA) reported spending more than US$1.2 billion on HIV and AIDS in 2009, of which US$750 million was spent in the Russian Federation. As the region assesses its progress toward universal access, it is reasonable to consider the return on that investment in making prevention, care and treatment services available to everyone.

Some progress has been made: prevention of vertical transmission coverage exceeds 90%; access to antiretroviral drugs is increasing although it remains among the lowest in the world; there has been progress in the legal systems on travel restrictions and harm-reduction in several countries; and public-sector spending on AIDS is rising. The recent Regional Consultation on Universal Access concluded, however, that the region's epidemic "remains serious" and "the burden of HIV is increasing".

Injecting drug users form a key population at higher risk in the sexual transmission of HIV, to their spouses and partners. Transmission also occurs via sex workers, and to a lesser but growing extent, through men who have sex with men (MSM). Prevention and treatment services are increasingly failing to reach them.

There are encouraging trends in harm-reduction policy making, but access to oral substitution services [for intravenous drug users] remains limited and often stigmatized. There are reports of harm-reduction services being denied; abuse of confidential drug-user registries; and police harassment and arbitrary arrests. HIV and tuberculosis (TB) coinfections are a particular concern in prisons, where multidrug resistant TB is

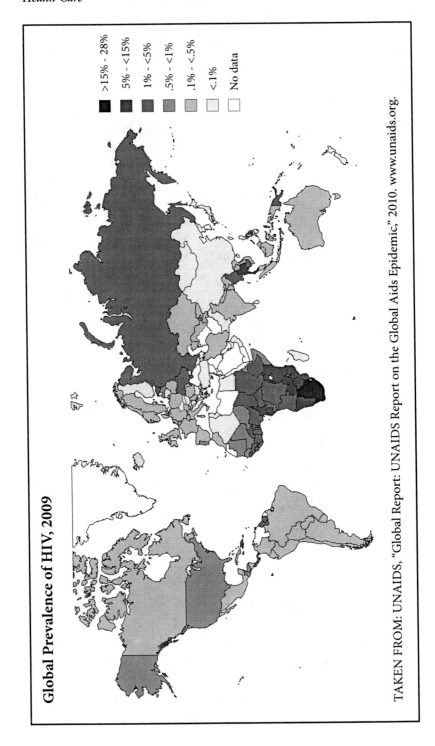

Global Prevalence of HIV, 2009

>15% - 28%
5% - <15%
1% - <5%
.5% - <1%
.1% - <.5%
<.1%
No data

TAKEN FROM: UNAIDS, "Global Report: UNAIDS Report on the Global Aids Epidemic," 2010. www.unaids.org.

common. Access to prevention and treatment for prisoners is low. Migrants have limited access to HIV prevention and treatment and lack health insurance coverage.

The region is home to a vigorous community of AIDS policy makers, researchers and activists. More than 150 high-ranking officials, experts and members of civil society gathered in Kiev for three days in March [2011] to assess their region's progress toward universal access and to set targets for 2015.

Cross-border collaboration between national governments remains insufficient and hampers initiatives for migrants. Civil society has assumed leadership and is willing to collaborate with governments, which sometimes adopt a confrontational rather than cooperative approach.

While some countries show progress, and a regional path toward universal access is emerging, most of the region's governments are not accelerating policies and programmes as epidemics worsen. That is particularly worrisome given that external aid will diminish as a result of reduced access to Global Fund grants.

Stronger policies, cost-effectiveness, bolder programming and political leadership are crucial to achieving a favourable return on investments. Investments to date are for the long term. Just how long depends on the pace at which the virus spreads compared with the pace at which governments respond.

HIV in Latin America

At first glance, statistics suggest HIV in Latin America is under control. Prevalence in the general population is stable at 0.4%. More than half the people needing treatment can receive it and universal access to treatment is a reality in Brazil, Costa Rica and Mexico. Costa Rica reported zero cases of vertical transmission in 2009.

But these numbers hide disparities. HIV prevalence is alarmingly high among men who have sex with men (MSM; up to 20.3%), sex workers (up to 19.3%) and transgender people (up to 34%), in some countries. Access to treatment is uneven, with difficulties particularly for key populations at risk, where stigma and discrimination continue to fuel the epidemic.

There is political will: 95% of the region's response to AIDS is funded by domestic resources, but allocations are not sufficiently aligned to the patterns of the epidemic, and funding for treatment far outweighs that for prevention, particularly among at-risk populations.

In 2006, Latin America was one of the first regions to commit to universal access when stakeholders gathered in Brazil to discuss scaling up HIV programmes.

To prepare for the second regional consultation in Mexico City in March 2011, 16 country-based technical reviews assessed progress against the 2006 targets. Findings were mixed: more MSM were getting tested, but young people were being diagnosed too late; generic antiretroviral drug production had increased but stock-outs were frequent; despite Costa Rica's success, there was no measurable improvement in preventing vertical transmission across the region; and data showed greater condom use among sex workers and more people who inject drugs using sterile equipment, but MSM still not being widely reached by prevention programmes promoting safer sex.

Unless every person in Latin America is able to access services without fear of reprisal or violence, access will not be universal. Ingrained social, cultural and economic barriers make women and girls and key populations at higher risk of infection. Initiatives that target men who have sex with men and transgender people must link to broader efforts that promote human rights and protect public health.

The region can be proud of its low HIV prevalence in the general population. Over the past 30 years, Latin America has kept infection rates low and services available, although strong efforts are still required to reach those most vulnerable to HIV. The 2006 and 2011 consultations demonstrate the region is responding to the epidemic's toughest challenges, and there is every reason to believe it has set the correct course.

With 1% prevalence, the Caribbean has the highest infection rate in the world after sub-Saharan Africa.

HIV in the Caribbean

With 1% prevalence, the Caribbean has the highest infection rate in the world after sub-Saharan Africa. Prevalence is highest among men who have sex with men (MSM) and sex workers, according to the most recent data. In Jamaica, 33% of MSM are living with HIV. In Suriname, 24% of female sex workers are infected with HIV.

With many Caribbean countries criminalizing sex work and sex between men, universal access will be impossible unless those laws change.

At the recent Regional Consultation on Universal Access in Trinidad and Tobago, leaders agreed those laws had to be repealed and revised. They called for a Pan-Caribbean Human Rights Charter to guarantee the right to health for all, a welcome united front against legalized discrimination. Following the consultation, the Jamaican Prime Minister and the Leader of the Opposition signed a "Declaration against HIV Stigma and Discrimination".

A review of the Caribbean AIDS epidemic offers good news and bad news. There was a 14% reduction in HIV incidence between 2001 and 2009—four countries reduced new HIV infections by 25%—and greater access to treatment reduced AIDS-related deaths by 43% over the same period. But

165

18,000 new infections took place in 2009, an average of 50 daily. Some 7000 women needed treatment to prevent vertical transmission but only 4000 received it. Most alarmingly, AIDS is the leading cause of death among Caribbeans aged 20–59.

In the past decade the Caribbean received more than US$1.8 billion in external funding. In 2009 external sources funded 64% of overall AIDS spending. As international development assistance diminishes, national investments must increase.

Regional leaders know they must think creatively and inclusively about new approaches. At the regional consultation in Trinidad and Tobago there was support for more women to assume leadership roles. If young men and women are to be reached, attention should be paid to the role of popular culture, education and links between HIV and sexual and reproductive health. Modernizing societal views on the key populations at higher risk requires innovation from new leaders. It is quite possible women will lead the way.

Ten years ago, HIV had no place on mainstream political or social agendas in the Middle East and North Africa.

The right of Caribbean people to make their own history was a resounding message at the consultation. It is up to the region's leaders to determine the role of AIDS in its history. AIDS could continue to decimate legally stigmatized populations, strain national budgets, and hurt industries. Caribbean societies need to make wiser investments and secure the needs and rights of all citizens.

HIV in the Middle East and North Africa

Ten years ago, HIV had no place on mainstream political or social agendas in the Middle East and North Africa, but today there is evidence that most countries in the region have changed course. In 2008, only eight countries contributed to multilateral progress reports; in 2010 that number was 20. All countries have developed national AIDS strategies, many using emerging evidence to shape their responses. All countries provide free antiretroviral drugs, yet more must be done to improve access to health services.

Stigma and discrimination against key populations at higher risk of infection still hamper progress toward universal access; a majority of countries in the region have laws that criminalize key populations. However, there have been improvements over the past five years. Egypt, Lebanon, Morocco and Tunisia have programmes targeting men who have sex with men, and sex workers. The Islamic Republic of Iran has adopted a combination prevention approach to reduce new HIV infections among people who inject drugs, while Djibouti has integrated migrant and mobile populations in its strategy.

The consensus statement from the Dubai consultation in June 2010 was a milestone in the region's response to HIV. Government and civil society representatives confronted controversial social and political issues, and committed to universal access to HIV prevention, treatment, care and support. They demanded an enabling environment that protects the human rights of vulnerable groups, including women and girls and people living with HIV. Participants agreed that people living with HIV and civil society should be better integrated into government policy making and programming.

The 16 government officials who signed the statement acknowledged that innovative financing initiatives, including domestic funding, were needed. The Global Fund is by far the region's largest donor (US$326.4 million over five years), and the percentage of HIV allocations in national budgets is still low overall, yet history shows progress depends on governments increasing domestic spending on the AIDS response.

The Declaration of Commitment and Call for Action endorsed at the Djibouti conference in September 2010 represented another major breakthrough, with participants calling for access to services for all mobile and migrant populations.

By endorsing the Dubai consensus statement, AIDS leaders in the Middle East and North Africa committed to integrating services; focusing on women and girls; combating stigma and discrimination; generating knowledge about epidemics and responses; developing innovative funding; fomenting an interministerial government response; building a strong civil society; and engaging in multilateral systems.

The Worldwide Fight Against Malaria Is Far from Over

Jeremy Laurance

In the following viewpoint, Jeremy Laurance argues that the incidence of malaria around the globe has been declining. Laurance contends this is due partly to the call for elimination of malaria by Bill Gates and the support of wealthy celebrities. Laurance claims that although there are many tools at hand for fighting malaria, past attempts have not always been successful. He raises concerns about the permanency of elimination and concludes the disease must be fought using several strategies, including a vaccine. Laurance is health editor for the Independent, *a newspaper in the United Kingdom.*

As you read, consider the following questions:

1. According to Laurance, what percentage of malaria cases occurs in sub-Saharan Africa?

2. How many countries in the world are free of malaria, according to the author?

3. According to Laurance, which seven African countries account for two-thirds of all malaria cases?

W hen I see a packet of malaria pills I think of that famous Clint Eastwood line from *Dirty Harry*, delivered as he pointed his .44 magnum at a bank robber and neither of them could remember how many shots he had fired, or whether there was still one left in the chamber. "The question you have got to ask yourself is: Do I feel lucky? Well, do ya, punk?"

Actually, I do. Lucky enough not to have to take the nasty, expensive little things on my periodic visits to Africa and other malarial parts of the world. Now I find myself being asked to reconsider after *X Factor* star Cheryl Cole's unpleasant encounter with a mosquito in Tanzania. Such is the power of celebrity.

A Decline in Malaria

I based my view on a *Lancet* paper published in the 1990s by London's Hospital for Tropical Diseases, which assessed the chances of contracting malaria, for those not taking prophylactic drugs, at 0.6 per cent for an average two-week holiday in East Africa. The authors described this as "high" and in public health terms I suppose it is—the Health Protection Agency points out that more than 1,500 people are diagnosed with malaria in the UK [United Kingdom] each year having acquired it abroad.

About 2.5 billion people live in malarial areas around the globe, and the disease kills almost a million of them every year, mostly children.

But it didn't seem high to me—and I disliked the way commercial travel clinics pushed expensive injections and other protective measures at frightened travellers without quantifying the risks. So for the last 15 years I have followed a rough rule of thumb: If I am slumming it or travelling into the bush, I take the pills; if I am staying in four-star hotels in town, I don't bother. My impression is that many regular visitors to Africa do the same. Public health doctors may demur—and Ms Cole's story undoubtedly strengthens their case.

She had spent only six days in Tanzania and had, reportedly, taken anti-malarial drugs that provide 90 per cent protection. How unlucky is that?

Doubly unlucky because—and this is the real story about malaria—in many parts of the world it is declining, rapidly. About 2.5 billion people live in malarial areas around the globe, and the disease kills almost a million of them every year, mostly children. Changes in the incidence of the disease may go unnoticed by tourists but have huge significance for the local population. Now Cheryl Cole, who first visited Tanzania last year on a charity expedition to Mount Kilimanjaro, has helped focus attention on their plight in a way she could hardly have anticipated.

In coastal Kenya, not far from where she was holidaying, cases of severe malaria in children have fallen 90 per cent in the last five years. Similar falls have been reported from other locations across Africa and the world.

In certain islands in the Philippines malaria has been eliminated. Mexico is said to be close to eradication, and some countries in Central and South America are moving in the same direction. Morocco was recently declared malaria-free by the World Health Organisation [WHO], helping boost the tourist trade there.

Sub-Saharan Africa, which bears 70 per cent of the disease burden, presents a much tougher challenge. Yet even here there have been spectacular advances, as in coastal Kenya. Last week [July 26, 2010], the African Leaders Malaria Alliance announced that malaria cases and deaths had been cut by up to 80 per cent in 10 African countries since 2000, including Ethiopia, Ghana, Rwanda, Zambia and Zanzibar.

The Call for Elimination

Among malaria specialists, where gloom prevailed a decade ago, the buzzword now is "elimination": no more malaria deaths by 2015 and no more malaria a decade or two after that. As the *Lancet* noted last month, "previously cautious malariologists, released from a 40-year collective depression . . . have been invigorated."

How has this change of heart come about? Some call it the Bill Gates effect. Almost three years ago, the world's biggest philanthropist threw down a challenge to the global health community to eliminate malaria in his lifetime. Sceptics responded that his dream would only be realised if he were cryo-preserved. Yet his call had a galvanising effect.

The foundation that he leads with his wife, Melinda, has not only given grants of dizzying size to the search for a malaria vaccine, the distribution of bed nets and other measures, it has also brought a new vigour to the entire aid industry. Its speed and flexibility leaves larger bureaucracies like the UN [United Nations] standing, and where it goes others follow. It has been described as a new type of multilateral organisation, introducing entrepreneurial flair to a sector submerged in red tape.

Some complain that Gates is seeking to replicate the world domination he achieved with Microsoft in another, albeit altruistic, sphere. These critics say the new entrepreneurial aid business he has spawned is undemocratic, overly powerful, and is leading to empire-building, wasteful competition, fragmentation and duplication. Why should Bill Gates decide which sorts of vaccines get developed? they ask.

There is no denying, however, the impact of Gates's interest on the bottom line. Today's funding for malaria, from all sources, exceeds $10bn (£6.3bn)—a hundredfold increase in little more than a decade. Celebrities from Senegalese musician Youssou N'Dour to David Beckham have joined the cause. Politicians Bill Clinton and Tony Blair have become involved through their respective aid foundations, followed by a growing queue of corporate donors and public figures who bring clout, profile and funding. This week, Andrew Mitchell, the International Development Secretary, published the UK's business plan for malaria, opening a consultation on the best ways of supporting the fight against the disease.

Malaria—for so long the poor relation to AIDS in terms of global attention, despite claiming more lives in many countries—is suddenly glamorous.

Today, 108 countries in the world are malaria-free.

Attempts at Controlling Malaria

The tools for elimination are at hand. More than 200m insecticide-treated bed nets have been distributed since 2000, and are estimated to have saved 1m lives, according to the Roll Back Malaria Partnership. Ban Ki-moon, the UN secretary-general, said that with the delivery of a further 150m bed nets by the end of this year "universal coverage of malaria prevention can be achieved". Vast funds have been invested in indoor spraying against mosquitoes, in distributing more effective artemesinin-based drugs against the disease, and in developing a vaccine, with one candidate, made by the UK-based pharmaceutical manufacturer GlaxoSmithKline, in final (phase III) human trials.

But meeting Gates's challenge will be a tough task. Optimists, such as Sir Richard Feachem of the Malaria Elimination Group, point to the "shrinking map" of malaria, which included the US and the UK in 1900 (when malaria was endemic in the Kent marshes). Today, 108 countries in the world are malaria-free. One hundred countries have continuing malaria transmission, and of these, 39 are embarked upon malaria elimination. The remaining 61 are striving to control malaria, but it is Feachem's hope that they too can be persuaded to switch to a policy of elimination.

The task is immense. In 2008, malaria killed 863,000 people. Almost 90 per cent of those who died were in Africa, and of those, almost 90 per cent were children under five, ac-

The Need for Many Tools

History has demonstrated that an overreliance on a small number of tools to combat malaria is dangerous. With the emerging spread of parasite resistance to antimalarial medicines and mosquito resistance to insecticides, the challenge is to develop an array of tools that do not rely too heavily on any one active ingredient, as resistance to that ingredient is likely to occur over time.

Bill & Melinda Gates Foundation,
"Malaria: Strategy Overview," www.gatesfoundation.org.

cording to the WHO. Children are especially vulnerable because they have undeveloped immune systems; the WHO estimates the disease kills 3,000 children a day.

The world has been striving to eliminate malaria for more than half a century—with faint success. The Global Malaria Eradication Programme was launched in 1955 but it quickly became apparent that its ambition was not achievable in sub-Saharan Africa. In the late sixties the strategy switched from eradication to long-term control; people with fever caused by the disease were treated with the then standard drug, chloroquine. But as resistance to the drug grew, malaria deaths rose through the 1970s and 1980s. By the early 1990s the strategy was recognised as a disaster.

Throughout the 1990s, as nations wrung their hands over AIDS, efforts were made to refocus attention on malaria. The world's health ministers launched a global declaration in Amsterdam in 1992 to control the disease, with a focus on Africa. The latest drive against the disease began 10 years ago, when leaders of countries across Africa signed a declaration in Abuja, Nigeria, to "halve the malaria mortality for Africa's people by 2010". Initially progress was slow; there were reports that instead of declining, malaria was rising, by up to half in some areas. Accurate figures were hard to come by, and estimates were distrusted. What is not in dispute, however, is that over the last three years things have moved much more quickly, and more consistently in the right direction. The huge rise in the importation of bed nets and artemesinin drugs has saved millions of lives.

Controlling malaria has come to be seen as good business, not just good charity. The disease is estimated to cost Africa $12bn a year—1.3 per cent of its economic growth. If that sum could be saved, it would constitute the biggest boost to health and development in the continent's history. Eradicating disease boosts productivity, creates markets and stabilises governments.

Malaria is concentrated around the equator ... with just seven countries accounting for two-thirds of all cases.

Challenges in Fighting Malaria

The future, however, is anything but certain. Though the 90 per cent fall in children with severe malaria on the Kenyan coast is impressive, the reasons are not obvious. Malaria has been in decline in this area for at least 15 years and some have suggested climate change is a factor. Meanwhile it is rising in upland areas around Mount Kenya, where incidence was previously low. Professor Robert Snow, who reported the Kenyan figures in the *Lancet*, said malaria had changed "from a major cause of childhood illness and death to a relatively minor problem" on Kenya's coast. But it was simplistic to attribute it to more bed nets and better drugs. "The truth is probably much more complex," he wrote.

Critics also question the notion of "universal coverage" with bed nets—expected in Ethiopia and southern Sudan this year and everywhere in early 2011. How many nets can you hang in a small hut occupied by a large family? Some older children are always likely to go without. There have been distribution problems too: The rush to freight in bed nets has left thousands of them sitting in warehouses because there was no means of transporting them over the final miles.

Malaria is concentrated around the equator, the "middle, wet bit" of Africa, with just seven countries accounting for two-thirds of all cases: the Democratic Republic of the Congo, Ethiopia, Kenya, Nigeria, southern Sudan, Tanzania and Uganda. While there have been gains in some, others such as Nigeria have done less well. With a population of 120 million, Nigeria contributes heavily to the global malaria burden.

Even where success has been achieved, there is no guarantee it will be permanent. Zanzibar, the island off Tanzania that has become a luxury tourist destination, has eliminated malaria twice before but each time it has been re-imported from the mainland. Kenya has also slipped back, and in the Congo the uncertainties multiply.

The best hope for the future is a vaccine.

Constant vigilance is essential. That requires stable, committed government. It is not always available. In Uganda, grants worth over $350m were suspended by the Global Fund over allegations of corruption (which are currently before the courts). In Tanzania a grant worth over $100m from the Global Fund was discovered unclaimed last year because it lacked a single signature.

Countries worst affected by the disease have been reluctant to buy the new artemesinin-based drugs because of their cost. At $1 to $2 a dose, they are 10 times more expensive than chloroquine. Though funded by aid programmes today, governments wonder for how long that funding will last. There are fears about resistance too, signs of which have emerged on the Thai-Cambodian border. If the artemesinin drugs lose their potency, there is nothing else immediately in the pharmaceutical locker.

The Best Hope for the Future

Eradication may be the only way to combat resistance. The most taxing question, however, and one which divides the malaria community, is what penalties may follow success? Chris Drakeley, director of the Malaria Centre at the London School of Hygiene and Tropical Medicine, points out that enormous funds are required to eliminate the last few cases of a disease—witness polio, still defying efforts to wipe it from the planet.

"If malaria drops down the Top 10 list of worst diseases, what justification is there for putting in vast resources to eliminate it? In a situation where malaria had been controlled to a low level for a decade, you would have a large group of children with no immunity to the disease. The impact of an outbreak could then be devastating. There is an argument that some level of malaria is quite good—it maintains a level of immunity in the population."

The best hope for the future is a vaccine. No disease has ever been eliminated without a vaccine. But malaria is not caused by a simple virus—it is an organism (a parasite) with a nucleus that is more complex than a virus.

The front runner is GlaxoSmithKline's RTSS vaccine, currently being tested in 14,000 children in 11 African countries, with results due in 2012. Early trials suggested that it provided 30–50 per cent protection—far from perfect, but a lot better than nothing.

Scientists are optimistic that it will provide a useful further weapon against malaria. But there will be many years yet of fighting before the war can be declared won.

Drug-Resistant Tuberculosis Poses a Global Health Threat

Jeneen Interlandi

In the following viewpoint, Jeneen Interlandi argues that the world faces a tipping point in dealing with tuberculosis (TB), where the disease threatens to become incurable. Interlandi claims drug-resistant TB has been showing up in nearly every country. Interlandi contends that part of the reason TB has developed resistance to antibiotics is that money has been spent on other diseases, such as HIV, rather than dealing with this growing problem. Interlandi warns that questions about how to spend money and how to fight the disease need to be answered quickly before it is too late. Interlandi is a reporter for Newsweek.

As you read, consider the following questions:

1. According to Interlandi, how many people die every day from tuberculosis?

2. A person with HIV is how many times more likely to develop tuberculosis, according to the author?

3. By the early 1990s HIV funding had become how many times greater than funding for tuberculosis, according to Interlandi?

It's been nearly a decade since U2 front man Bono turned the entire continent of Africa into a pet cause, drawing attention to the problems of developing-world health like never before. By some accounts, that publicity has started to pay off: Since 2000, malaria incidence is down 50 percent in some of the hardest-hit regions, and in the past five years, the number of people with access to lifesaving HIV medications has increased tenfold. But while First World philanthropists and rock-star do-gooders were out to conquer AIDS and malaria, they left a far more ancient killer to fester. Tuberculosis has been traced back as far as the Egyptian mummies. It still kills 5,000 people every day—more people than swine flu has killed in the past year. And right now, natural selection and human fallibility are conspiring to make the germ indestructible.

The Rise of Drug-Resistant Tuberculosis

Since the first effective medications were made available in 1944, *Mycobacterium tuberculosis* has routinely developed resistance to one drug after another. But in the late 1990s a more disturbing trend emerged: Strains of tuberculosis [TB] called multidrug-resistant, or MDR-TB, that were resistant to not one but several of the most effective medications (called first-line drugs), began popping up in Africa, Asia, and Eastern Europe. Now those strains have evolved into something even more deadly: extensively drug-resistant, or XDR-TB, which is impervious to first-, second-, and third-line drugs— virtually all the antibiotics in existence. It's the kind of bug that gives epidemiologists nightmares. And in the past two years [2008–2009], while the world was distracted by the financial crisis, it has emerged in nearly every country on the planet. Experts say it's time to start worrying. In a 2009 speech delivered to the U.N. [United Nations], World Health Organization [WHO] director Margaret Chan warned that without swift, decisive action, we might soon find ourselves back in "an era that predates the development of antibiotics," when tuberculosis was completely incurable. In country after country, drug-resistant strains will start to replace drug-susceptible strains, spreading from the inner cities to the suburbs and from the slums to the countryside. And as scientists start from scratch in a hunt for effective antibiotics, the death toll will steadily rise in rich countries as well as poor.

Right now, natural selection and human fallibility are conspiring to make the germ indestructible.

The global health community is scrambling. In April 2009, at an emergency meeting in Beijing, experts acknowledged the situation was a disaster in the making, but said that reversing course would be impossible without a huge influx of cash. It's true that new medications, modern diagnostics, and more and better-trained doctors and nurses are urgently needed, and that those things will cost money. But a small contingent of TB specialists has begun to argue that money will not be enough. What's really needed, they say, is a whole new way of doing business—a way that apportions funding based on need, not just Western interests. Western dollars have skewed global health priorities in favor of diseases with young victims, obvious solutions, or a good "Nobel Prize–worthy" challenge. Tuberculosis has thrived by sidestepping any such attention—capturing snags. It's old. It preys on societies' most disenfranchised members. And having made an ally of the very air we breathe, it won't be deterred by anything as simple as a condom or a bed net. In fact, experts say that more than any other disease, this 19th-century relic is exposing all the cracks in our multibillion-dollar global health system.

HIV and Tuberculosis

Roughly one-third of humanity carries a latent form of tuberculosis: thick, encrusted capsules deep within the lungs that were formed when the immune system first encountered the

Worldwide Incidence of Multidrug-Resistant Tuberculosis (MDR-TB)

In 2008, an estimated 390,000–510,000 cases of MDR-TB [multidrug-resistant tuberculosis] emerged globally (best estimate, 440,000 cases). Among all incident TB cases globally, 3.6% are estimated to have MDR-TB. . . . Almost 50% of MDR-TB cases worldwide are estimated to occur in China and India. In 2008, MDR-TB caused an estimated 150,000 deaths.

World Health Organization,
"Multidrug and Extensively Drug-Resistant TB (M/XDR-TB):
2010 Global Report on Surveillance and Response," 2010.

bacteria and fought them to a stalemate. In healthy people, those capsules can remain dormant for decades; most people go their entire lives without ever knowing they're infected. But when the immune system is compromised—as it is with HIV—the capsules burst open and the bacteria begin a slow, consumptive feast of lung, kidney, bone, and neuron known as active TB. Someone with HIV is 20 to 30 times more likely to develop active TB, so when this unknown retrovirus reached epidemic proportions in the late 1980s, the ancient bacteria were not far behind.

At the time, global health experts were focused on improving primary care around the world, convinced that would be the key to eliminating disease. People with clean water, nutritious food, and functioning clinics, they reasoned, would be less likely to spread illness in the first place and better able to withstand the outbreaks that did occur. The approach held particular promise for combating tuberculosis, a disease that was thriving in places with poor sanitation and rampant malnutrition. But as the AIDS epidemic swelled, wealthy nations began flooding the developing world with their cash, expertise, and good intentions. Before long, priorities shifted. Food, water, and basic infrastructure fell by the wayside; vaccine development, drug discovery, and the eradication of individual diseases became paramount. By accident, a new global health system was born, one in which every parasite was a cause unto itself, and some causes—namely those that captured the Western imagination—were bigger than others.

In this new paradigm, TB experts and HIV experts found themselves pitted against one another in a quest for attention, funding, and intellectual capital. Thanks largely to activism in wealthy countries, the HIV team won out: By the early 1990s, HIV funding was five times greater than TB funding. But even as it became clear that the epidemics were linked, the AIDS boon did not lead to progress on TB. HIV workers were trained in TB control only as an afterthought; labs built with HIV money were not equipped to diagnose or treat TB. And as the arsenal of anti-HIV medications grew tenfold, the number of tuberculosis drugs remained abysmal. Before long, tuberculosis had emerged as the single biggest killer of people with HIV-AIDS, and HIV-positive populations in Africa and Asia had become hotbeds of drug-resistant TB.

Roughly one-third of humanity carries a latent form of tuberculosis.

The Tipping Point

As these newer, deadlier strains began to emerge in disparate regions—from Africa and Asia to Eastern Europe and the United States—experts found themselves divided over how to proceed. Some wanted to treat the problem aggressively—using available funds to treat as many drug-resistant cases as possible so that XDR-TB would not spread. But second-line drugs are far more expensive than first-line drugs, and many scientists believed that the drug-resistance problem would eventually take care of itself. Any mutation that rendered a given strain of the microbe drug-resistant would also make that strain more virulent, they thought. The more virulent a strain became, the faster it would kill its host and the less time it would have to spread through the population. "The hope was that the resistant strains would just fizzle out over time," says Salmaan Keshavjee, a Harvard Medical School physician who works on TB control in Africa and Eastern Europe with the nonprofit Partners in Health. "But that didn't happen." As Keshavjee and his colleagues discovered, even XDR-TB patients who face mortality rates as high as 90 percent usually live for several months—more than enough time to pass the bug along.

Because XDR-TB patients live to infect others, ignoring the problem now will most certainly cost us more later. Reversing course will require an aggressive offense, and that will mean spending more money up front on developing drugs and diagnostics and making them available to the people who need them. But money is only part of the problem, and it may not even be the biggest part. Fighting XDR-TB will require wholesale changes in the global health system: TB and HIV specialists will have to work together. More resources will have to be devoted to primary care. And wealthy countries will have to pay attention to tuberculosis.

We are headed for a tipping point. In some pockets of the world, XDR strains are on track to replace drug-susceptible strains in the coming years. This is already happening in parts of Russia—the number of drug-resistant cases has doubled even as the number of drug-susceptible cases remains flat. "It means we really could end up in a situation where tuberculosis is completely incurable," says Mario Raviglione, director of the WHO's Stop TB program. When that happens, it may truly be too late.

India on the Front Lines in the Battle to Eradicate Polio

Stephanie Nolen

In the following viewpoint, Stephanie Nolen argues that India is on the brink of eliminating polio. However, she claims that there is a danger of the disease coming back if efforts to eradicate polio are not continued. Nolen contends that polio vaccination in India has quickly reduced the number of cases of polio. However, she notes that the disease still remains and can flare up very quickly without vigilance. Nolen is a foreign correspondent for the Globe and Mail, *the national newspaper of Canada. She is author of* 28: Stories of AIDS in Africa.

As you read, consider the following questions:

1. According to Nolen, software tycoon Bill Gates has spent how much on polio eradication in a recent three-year period?

2. The wild polio virus has survived in which two poor northern India states, according to the author?

3. According to Nolen, besides India and Nigeria, in what two other countries is polio endemic?

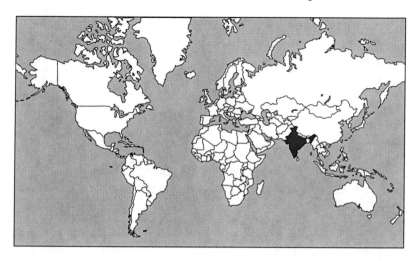

Through the heaving crowd of a Delhi railway platform, Vandana Saini spots a sleeping toddler slumped on her mother's shoulder. She darts forward brandishing a tiny squeeze bottle. "Polio?" she hollers over the screech of train brakes, inspecting the baby's fingernail for the tell-tale ink mark that shows the recently vaccinated. The mother shrinks back for a moment, then recognizes Ms. Saini's yellow vest, the sign of India's 2.3-million volunteer vaccinators. She nods assent and tips the baby's head off her shoulder. As the crowd eddies around them, Ms. Saini expertly squeezes the baby's cheeks until her mouth opens, deposits two drops of vaccine, marks the fingernail and sends the family onward, pivoting on her heel to spot the next child.

She will squeeze and drop, squeeze and drop each day this week, as she has tens of thousands of times before in her 10 years of working with India's polio eradication effort. She patrols the platforms and she rides the trains, working her way from car to car until she has done all the children, then disembarks and gets started on the next train back—seven or eight trains in a day.

This way, the polio team hopes, she will catch impoverished economic migrants flooding into the city. They come from villages with no sanitation to slums with no sanitation and they are most likely to carry the virus and be missed in a door-to-door campaign. An army of volunteers is at work this week at every rail station, every bus depot, every major cross-road outside the megacities; they aim to inoculate 174 million children.

The train-station campaigns are an Indian innovation, one of several new approaches that have helped to get this country achingly close to a goal that has seemed, for years, unobtainable.

Polio is all but gone from India, from this gigantic nation that has been the source for most of the critical new outbreaks in recent years, its last stand winnowed down to just two or three areas no bigger than 30 square kilometres.

Polio is all but gone from India, from this gigantic nation that has been the source for most of the critical new outbreaks in recent years.

"We have it on the ropes," said Bruce Aylward, the Canadian who has directed the World Health Organization's global polio eradication program for more than a decade.

Yet India's moment has gone unnoticed by a world bored with the "this-close" narrative of polio. This has critical implications: The fight against polio is all but bankrupt—short of $720-million (all figures U.S.) for 2011–12, despite hearty promises from G8 countries to keep the effort well funded to the end.

A high-powered partnership has formed around polio eradication in recent years, its great new champion software tycoon Bill Gates, who calls this ambition his "number one priority" and whose foundation has put in $760 million in the last three years. And the WHO, UNICEF and Rotary International are equally engaged. India itself injects $300 million a year into the fight. But without the cash to continue, the partnership will have to curtail efforts to boost coverage.

Dr. Aylward and other experts understand the donor frustration—year after year, polio cases decline in some countries, but swell in others, while the overall cost of the campaign nears $10 billion. "The program seemed to stall on the precipice of eradication," said Hamid Jafari, the director of the WHO's India team.

But the experts have a worry of their own: This time, it really is different. India has had just one polio case in 2011, and only six in the past six months. And if it's possible here, "You can do it anywhere," Dr. Jafari said.

Before the eradication campaign, India saw as many as 50,000 to 100,000 cases a year.

India's fight against polio holds two lessons for the rest of the world: The first concerns the perils of getting close to wiping out the virus, but not all the way there—and the second, the progress that is possible with a combination of political will, a healthy budget and scientific and social innovation. The poliomyelitis virus, which can cause life-threatening paralysis in just hours, was once a global scourge.

After Jonas Salk found a vaccine in 1953, fears of polio began to ebb in the developed world; a global eradication effort began in 1988, and the virus was gone from the Americas in 1991. By 1999, it remained only in a handful of countries in central and south Asia and Africa.

Before the eradication campaign, India saw as many as 50,000 to 100,000 cases a year, but by 2005, it was down to just 66. But as the number waned, so did vigilance. The virus resurged the following year with 676 cases—many of them Indians who migrated . . . taking the virus back into areas where it had long been eradicated, or abroad.

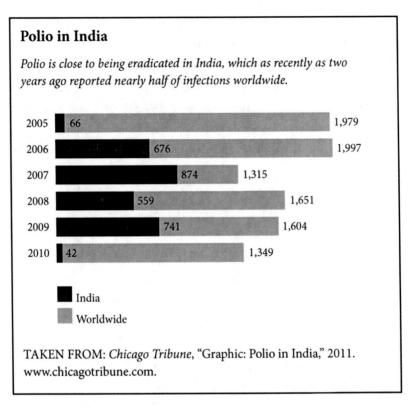

Polio in India

Polio is close to being eradicated in India, which as recently as two years ago reported nearly half of infections worldwide.

Year	India	Worldwide
2005	66	1,979
2006	676	1,997
2007	874	1,315
2008	559	1,651
2009	741	1,604
2010	42	1,349

■ India
▨ Worldwide

TAKEN FROM: *Chicago Tribune*, "Graphic: Polio in India," 2011. www.chicagotribune.com.

Microbiologists can "fingerprint" a virus and tell, based on its genetic makeup, where it came from—right down to the neighbourhood.

So we know that a 2007 outbreak in Angola, which had been polio-free, came from India. Then the virus spilled over the Angolan border into the Democratic Republic of the Congo and then Congo-Brazzaville—two countries from which polio had been chased out, but where weak public-health systems and low vaccination coverage made it difficult to contain the new epidemics.

Meanwhile, two reservoirs of wild polio virus survived here: one in western Uttar Pradesh, the other in central Bihar. These two states in northern India are among the poorest and most populated. Some 500,000 new babies are born in Uttar Pradesh every single month, yet less than half of these are born in medical facilities where they might get the vaccine. In Bihar, the virus lurks in the Kosi River floodplains—a teeming area where people live with little or no access to basic sanitation services or public health.

Dr. Jafari sends teams of vaccinators on motorbikes into the river delta, where they heave the bikes onto small boats to move between communities and then trek from each village eight or 10 kilometres out to a barsa, where people keep children in rough lean-tos to help stake a claim to land recently flooded with fertile silt. All the way, they lug ice chests with the vaccine, which quickly breaks down at room temperature. "There are more than a million children under the age of five on the Kosi River embankment alone," he said.

The fight is not over in India.

Teams infiltrated the most inaccessible areas, and repeatedly vaccinated more than 90 per cent of children. In most places, that is enough to quash polio, but not in Kosi or Uttar Pradesh. "Here you need at least 95 per cent—in an area with extremely high population density and zero public services," Dr. Aylward said. "It's like having to run the 100 meters two seconds faster than anyone else in the Olympics."

No one knows why the vaccine works only half as well in these areas. The extremely high levels of diarrhea in children? The profusion of other bugs in their gut? But they needed a new plan.

Polio comes in three distinct strains. The vaccine used in most of the world targets all three. In northern India, that vaccine wiped out type 2, but didn't work as well on 1 or 3. So the polio campaign decided to revert to type-specific vaccines used in the early days of immunization. But whenever they drove type 1 back, 3 flared up; when they quashed 3, then 1 came back. Dr. Jafari likened it to a vicious game of Ping-Pong.

This called for a new vaccine, one that would work against types 1 and 3 simultaneously, without, in lay terms, cancelling each other out.

Normally the production of a new vaccine would be years in the making. But the WHO teamed up with India's Council for Medical Research and local pharmaceutical firms to design a vaccine that worked on types 1 and 3—and they were using it on children in just six months. "The commitment of the government of India and the state governments is incredible—India is the only country that funds more than 80 per cent of its polio program," Dr. Jafari said.

The Indian government reported just 42 cases last year—down 94 per cent from the year before, and the lowest number ever recorded here.

That news is, in a way, even better than it sounds: In the entire high-transmission season, which comes with the summer monsoon, there was not a single case in Uttar Pradesh, and just three in Bihar. From nine distinct genetic clusters of type 1 polio virus in 2006, there is now just one.

"We've never been this close," Dr. Jafari said, his voice lowered, as if not to tempt fate. "We've never seen this picture before."

India will need to maintain the rounds of mass vaccination for a few years, to keep herd immunity high.

That said, the fight is not over in India: There was an unexpected, fast-moving outbreak in West Bengal last year caused by a virus from Bihar. But an extensive "mop-up operation" is under way there now, before the rains come, and if no new cases are reported for 18 months, India will be removed from the list of four countries where polio remains endemic.

One of the holdouts is Nigeria, which had a sharp flare-up in cases after 2003. In Nigeria, state governments banned vaccination when rumours spread that the polio vaccine was actually being used to sterilize Muslims. The virus spread from Nigeria back into 12 countries that had wiped it out. Heavy lobbying persuaded Islamic leaders to urge people to cooperate with vaccinators. Nigeria reported just 21 cases in 2010, down from 388 cases in 2009. Experts believe eradication may be possible there soon.

The last two endemic countries are Afghanistan and Pakistan. Despite the weak state and vicious fighting in much of Afghanistan, a team there has successfully negotiated with warring factions to allow access to children.

India will need to maintain the rounds of mass vaccination for a few years, to keep herd immunity high—and also redouble efforts at surveillance, so that if a new case pops up, it is caught immediately.

The surveillance network investigates all reported cases of acute flaccid paralysis, the tell-tale sign of polio—some 55,000 a year.

The WHO team regularly reminds doctors in hospitals and private practice to call their hotline the moment they see a limp-limbed child. It also cultivates relationships with herbalists, village healers and temple priests, to whom poor people often take sick children first.

The cause is not without dedicated backers: Mohammed bin Zayed Al Nahyan, the crown prince of Abu Dhabi, recently pledged $50 million to vaccinate children in Pakistan and Afghanistan, while the Gates Foundation has pledged another $450 million for the next two years.

But, Dr. Aylward said, it isn't enough: They need the world's richest nations to pitch in further. In 2005 (and many times since), the G8 member countries pledged to maintain or increase their contributions, yet G8 contributions for 2011–12 account for just 12 per cent of the global campaign's $1.86-billion budget, compared with 58 per cent in 2004–05.

Walter Orenstein, a polio expert with the Gates Foundation, called this the greatest threat: that in an era of economic downturn, donors will think that almost eradicating polio sounds good enough. "We will get periods of silence," he warned. "And then outbreaks like in the Congo or Tajikistan."

The budget shortfall means that Dr. Aylward is "cutting corners" in vaccine rounds in Nigeria, scaling back a vaccination campaign in the Congo and restricting surveillance in India. It's risky. And if the disease isn't wiped out, he said, when the world came this close, it will stand as a stark rebuttal to the idea that all children are created equal. "If we don't end polio now, we're not saying it's because we can't, we're saying, 'It ain't worth it.' Because now, we have no excuse. Now we know it's doable."

Infectious Diseases in the Developing World Remain a Serious Problem

*International Federation of Red Cross
and Red Crescent Societies (IFRC)*

*In the following viewpoint, the International Federation of Red
Cross and Red Crescent Societies (IFRC) argues that despite the
fact that noncommunicable diseases take more lives, communicable diseases pose a grave threat in developing countries. IFRC
claims that the social and economic impacts of infectious diseases
are huge in poor countries and are hindering development. In
addition, IFRC claims that infectious disease epidemics in developing countries pose a threat to the entire world. IFRC is the
world's largest humanitarian organization, providing assistance
without discrimination as to nationality, race, religious beliefs,
class, or political opinions.*

As you read, consider the following questions:

1. According to the International Federation of Red Cross
   and Red Crescent Societies (IFRC), neglected, emerging,
   and re-emerging diseases affect what fraction of the
   world's population?

2. How many people in the world suffer from dengue fever
   each year, according to the IFRC?

3. The IFRC claims that the Measles Initiative reduced global measles deaths by what percentage between 2000
and 2007?

Infectious diseases still cause close to 14 million deaths every
year. Respiratory infections account for four million deaths
annually, with more than two million deaths for diarrhoeal
diseases out of a total of 4.5 billion episodes estimated every
year. Meningitis kills half of the people that are infected. This
is more than 340,000 deaths. Nine million cases of dengue fever are also recorded every year and yet, this rarely hits the
news.

Meanwhile, neglected, emerging and re-emerging diseases
affect approximately one in six of the world's population and
more than 70 per cent of countries affected are low-income or
lower-income countries.

Looking Beyond Mortality Rates

These statistics speak for themselves and emphasize the grav-
ity of the situation. However, experts will argue that if you
take into consideration the mortality rate alone, noncommunicable diseases (such as cancer and heart conditions) have
become the leading cause of deaths worldwide. Since 2004,
they have been responsible for six in ten deaths compared to
three in ten for communicable, reproductive or nutritional
conditions and one in ten for injuries. But relying on the
mortality rate can be misleading, as it does not take into account other key components that need to be included.

The use of other indicators instead of just the number of
deaths will allow the data to disclose the real picture of the serious effect communicable diseases have on the community.
When it comes to evaluating the real burden of diseases, other
aspects such as the age in which the death happens need to be
taken into account.

For instance, a 70-year-old man dying of a heart attack in
Switzerland will lose an average of nine years of life if you

take into account life expectancy at birth for a male is 79. Because he is retired, used his skills, had the opportunity to raise his family and send his children to school, the social and economic effects of his death will be less severe.

Now let's take the example of a 20-year-old student who dies of cholera in Mozambique. Even though life expectancy at birth is much more limited, at 48 years, the social and economic consequences will be more serious. His community will not benefit from the education that he received at school, he will not be in the position to take care of his parents, younger brothers and sisters as this is traditionally the case in Africa. If he lives in a village, he will no longer be able to cultivate his land. The well-being of the community and the economic development of a country can therefore be hindered by the effects of epidemics and this is not demonstrated if only the mortality rate is taken into account.

Without taking into account the longer-term health, social, cultural and economical consequences of epidemics, their full effect cannot be sufficiently calculated or understood.

Another interesting parameter is the disabling effects of communicable disease. Let's take the example of a two-year-old girl who becomes paralyzed due to polio infection. Polio may not kill her but it will render her disabled for life, possibly preventing her from going to school, finding a job, cultivating the land or having a family. Furthermore, this child will need expensive human and material resources to care for her for the rest of her life. Even if she dies at the age of 60, her life will be made difficult as well as for those in the community who will need to support her. In this case, instead of spending a few cents to vaccinate the child, the family, community and government will have to bear the social and economical brunt of caring for her disability.

As illustrated, without taking into account the longer-term health, social, cultural and economical consequences of epidemics, their full effect cannot be sufficiently calculated or understood.

The Social and Economic Consequences

Communicable diseases are the enemies of development. The vicious circle of disease and low resources needs to be broken if development goals are to be reached. Besides the devastating effects of chronic communicable diseases on wealth and development as seen with HIV and tuberculosis, other epidemics claim their fair share of destruction of livelihoods in the poorest and most vulnerable communities.

We rarely hear of dengue fever, which causes a relatively low mortality of 18,000 people every year. However, when looking beyond the bare figures, we will be able to see the burden of nine million cases of dengue on communities that cannot continue their normal life due to sickness, overwhelmed health facilities, and absenteeism.

One of the major dangers facing the international community when dealing with epidemics is complacency, especially in developed countries.

The World Bank estimates that dengue fever—which is widely spread in Africa, the Americas, eastern Mediterranean, Southeast Asia and west Pacific—causes severe social and economical burdens.

For instance, the burden of dengue in Puerto Rico alone during 1984–1994 was similar to that for the entire Latin America and Caribbean region from malaria, tuberculosis, intestinal helminths, and other childhood diseases.

A Worldwide Threat

One of the major dangers facing the international community when dealing with epidemics is complacency, especially in developed countries. There is sometimes the idea that communicable diseases are now only a problem for developing countries because of the tremendous progress that has been made in medicine and the growing number of modern and sophisticated healthcare facilities. However, recent history showed us that there is a need to remain vigilant even in developed countries.

Measles is a good example of why we should not lower our guard. Many efforts have been made to reduce measles-related morbidity and mortality, especially in Africa, with tremendous success. Between 2000 and 2007, the Measles Initiative (led by the American Red Cross, the United Nations Foundation, the US Centers for Disease Control and Prevention, UNICEF [United Nations Children's Fund] and WHO [World Health Organization]) managed to slash the number of measles deaths in Africa by 89 per cent, which represents a considerable achievement and a major contribution to the UN [United Nations] Millennium Development Goals. Thousands of Red Cross and Red Crescent volunteers were involved in immunization campaigns, mobilising communities and convincing families to bring their children to vaccination centres. The number of lives that have been saved is equal to a reduction in global measles deaths by 74 per cent, from an estimated 750,000 deaths in 2000 to 197,000 in 2007. This is arguably the biggest public health success since the eradication of smallpox and should be followed for other communicable diseases.

Yet, as the international community was celebrating this major accomplishment, measles cases reappeared in Britain and Switzerland due to a lapse in routine immunization. This came as a necessary reminder that there is a need to be constantly vigilant and to maintain the required levels of immunization so that diseases such as measles do not reemerge.

Cancer Is a Growing Health Problem, Especially in the Developing World

Margaret Chan and Yukiya Amano

In the following viewpoint, Margaret Chan and Yukiya Amano argue that cancer is a public health problem worldwide, but it is now placing the greatest burden on impoverished countries. Chan and Amano claim that there is little infrastructure in place in the developing world for preventing, screening, or treating cancer, leading to many unnecessary deaths. Chan and Amano conclude that there needs to be a worldwide effort to control cancer in the developing world. Chan is director general of the World Health Organization, and Amano is director general of the International Atomic Energy Agency.

As you read, consider the following questions:

1. According to Chan and Amano, the number of cancer deaths in the developing world is forecast to grow to what number by 2015?

2. The authors claim that what fraction of cancers can be prevented?

3. Chan and Amano call for a concerted global action against cancer similar to the successful mobilization against what other disease?

Cancer is an enormous—and growing—global public health problem. And, of the 7.6 million cancer deaths every year, 4.8 million occur in the developing world. A disease formerly considered more pervasive in affluent countries now places its heaviest burden on poor and disadvantaged populations.

Cancer in the Developing World

In some African countries, fewer than 15% of cancer patients survive for five years following diagnosis of cervical and breast cancer, diseases that are highly curable elsewhere in the world. These are shocking statistics, with huge implications for human suffering, health care systems (and budgets), and the international drive to reduce poverty. So they should be treated as a call to action.

The increase in cancer's impact on the poor reflects factors such as demographic growth, population aging, the spread of unhealthy lifestyles (including tobacco use), and lack of control of cancer-associated infections. Though many cancers develop slowly, lifestyle changes take place with stunning speed and reach. These trends are not easily reversed.

A disease formerly considered more pervasive in affluent countries now places its heaviest burden on poor and disadvantaged populations.

If no action is taken, the number of cancer deaths in the developing world is forecast to grow to 5.9 million in 2015 and 9.1 million in 2030. While cancer deaths in wealthy countries are expected to increase less dramatically, they are nonetheless predicted to rise by a harrowing 40% over the next 20 years.

Throughout the developing world, most health care systems are designed to cope with episodes of infectious disease. But most lack the funds, equipment, and qualified personnel needed to provide basic care for cancer patients. Thirty countries—half of them in Africa—do not have a single radiotherapy machine. And these countries certainly do not have the financial resources, facilities, equipment, technology, infrastructure, staff, or training to cope with the long-term demands of cancer care.

They also have little capacity for prevention, public education, or early diagnosis and treatment, whether it be early detection in primary care, surgery, radiotherapy, or chemotherapy. In large parts of Africa, such treatments are usually reserved for those rich enough to seek specialized care abroad.

The demands of chronic care for a disease like cancer are simply overwhelming. Countries and families also pay a huge economic cost, as the lives of millions of people who could otherwise have made productive contributions to their families and communities for many decades are cut short.

The real tragedy, of course, is that many of these patients do not have to die. We know that around one-third of cancers can be prevented. This figure could be increased markedly if more emphasis were placed on identifying additional environmental and lifestyle-associated factors that increase cancer risks. In addition, a diagnosis no longer has to be a death sentence, because one-third of cancers can be cured if detected early and treated properly.

Global Cancer Control

The World Health Organization [WHO] and the International Atomic Energy Agency [IAEA] are working closely together to improve cancer control in developing countries. The IAEA's work involves building countries' capacity for radiation medicine. But technology means nothing without well-trained and motivated staff to use it. That is why both organizations are developing training and mentoring networks and innovative public-private partnerships. With its broad approach to public health, it is also essential to strengthen health care systems and primary care in order to improve early detection, timely diagnosis and treatment, as well as palliative care.

Preventive measures such as public health initiatives to curb smoking can be remarkably effective. Vaccines against hepatitis B and human papillomavirus, if made available at affordable prices, could contribute significantly to the prevention of liver and cervical cancers, respectively. At the International Agency for Research on Cancer, the specialized cancer agency of WHO, further research on the causes of cancer is being conducted, which promises to provide the base of evidence required to alleviate even more of the worldwide cancer burden.

Cancer should be acknowledged as a vital part of the global health agenda.

We are seeing promising results in individual countries, but our efforts are just a drop in a vast ocean of need. In order to respond to the growing cancer epidemic, we need nothing less than concerted global action similar to the successful mobilization against HIV/AIDS.

Cancer should be acknowledged as a vital part of the global health agenda. World leaders should be made aware of the scale of the cancer crisis facing developing countries. We need systematic action at the highest level to end the deadly disparity in cancer survival rates between rich and poor countries, thereby helping to save millions of lives. The goal must be to promote effective cancer control that is integrated into national health care systems throughout the developing world.

The United Nations General Assembly's Summit on Non-Communicable Diseases in September [2011] provides an opportunity to focus the world's attention on cancer in developing countries. Let us make cancer control one of the good news stories of 2011.

Periodical and Internet Sources Bibliography

The following articles have been selected to supplement the diverse views presented in this chapter.

Mike Barrett	"Counting Malaria Out," *New Statesman*, April 23, 2009.
Roger Bate	"Stifling Dissent on Malaria," *American*, December 8, 2008. www.american.com.
Tony Blair and Ray Chambers	"The Good Fight Against Malaria," *Project Syndicate*, April 22, 2011. www.project -syndicate.org.
Awa Marie Coll-Seck	"A Malaria-Free World Is Within Reach," *Global Health*, Summer 2011.
Andrew Jack	"World's Best Chance to Tackle Killer," *Financial Times*, April 23, 2009.
Ban Ki-moon and Margaret Chan	"Beyond Pandemics," *Project Syndicate*, June 15, 2009. www.project-syndicate.org.
Soumita Majumdar	"Infertility Problem Could Be Because of Tuberulosis," *Daily News and Analysis* (India), June 17, 2011.
David Molyneux	"The Forgotten Sick," *Project Syndicate*, April 26, 2010. www.project-syndicate.org.
Vineeta Pandey	"New Vaccine Gives Polio a Body Blow in India," *Daily News and Analysis* (India), July 27, 2010.
World Health Organization	"World Malaria Report 2010," 2010. www .who.int.

For Further Discussion

Chapter 1

1. The Kaiser Family Foundation argues that there are a large number of Americans without health insurance. According to the Organisation for Economic Co-operation and Development (OECD), how does health care coverage in the United States compare to other developed countries?

2. Based on the viewpoints of Y. Balarajan, S. Selvaraj, and S.V. Subramanian, regarding India, and Veronica M. Valdez, regarding China, what demographic faces similar problems in accessing health care in both India and China?

Chapter 2

1. Matt Welch argues that overall he prefers the French health care system. On what point, however, does he appear to agree with Scott W. Atlas about the superiority of US health care?

2. According to the *Spectator* (UK) and Anita Raghavan, what challenge do Great Britain and Germany both face with respect to the future of their respective health care systems?

Chapter 3

1. Reviewing the viewpoints in this chapter, identify the most common economic challenges facing health care systems. How do these challenges vary across countries?

Chapter 4

1. According to the authors of the viewpoints in this chapter what challenges are common in fighting AIDS, malaria, tuberculosis, and polio, and what challenges are unique to each disease?

2. The International Federation of Red Cross and Red Crescent Societies (IFRC) argues that infectious diseases in developing countries need to be controlled, whereas Margaret Chan and Yukiya Amano stress the importance of fighting cancer in the developing world. Given limited health care funding, explain why fighting either infectious diseases or cancer takes priority. Defend your answer.

Organizations to Contact

The editors have compiled the following list of organizations concerned with the issues debated in this book. The descriptions are derived from materials provided by the organizations. All have publications or information available for interested readers. The list was compiled on the date of publication of the present volume; the information provided here may change. Be aware that many organizations take several weeks or longer to respond to inquiries, so allow as much time as possible.

Cato Institute
1000 Massachusetts Avenue NW
Washington, DC   20001-5403
(202) 842-0200 • fax: (202) 842-3490
website: www.cato.org

The Cato Institute is a public policy research foundation dedicated to limiting the role of government, protecting individual liberties, and promoting free markets. Cato has been a longtime advocate of deregulating the health care industry so that consumers can afford the health care insurance and treatment of their choice. Among the institute's publications is the book *Healthy Competition: What's Holding Back Health Care and How to Free It.*

Center for American Progress
1333 H Street NW, 10th Floor, Washington, DC   20005
(202) 682-1611 • fax: (202) 682-1867
website: www.americanprogress.org

The Center for American Progress is a nonprofit, nonpartisan organization dedicated to improving the lives of Americans through progressive ideas and action. The center dialogues with leaders, thinkers, and citizens to explore the vital issues facing America and the world. The Center for American

Progress publishes numerous research papers, which are available at its website, including "Quality Health Care Delivered Effectively and Efficiently."

Centre for Economic Policy Research (CEPR)

77 Bastwick Street, London   EC1V 3PZ
   United Kingdom
(44) 20 7183 8801 • fax: (44) 20 7183 8820
e-mail: cepr@cepr.org
website: www.cepr.org

The Centre for Economic Policy Research (CEPR) is the leading European research network in economics. CEPR conducts research through a network of academic outlets and disseminates the results to the private sector and policy community. CEPR produces a wide range of reports, books, and conference volumes each year, including "Patient Mobility, Health Care Quality and Welfare."

Global Health Council

1111 Nineteenth Street NW, Suite 1120
Washington, DC   20036
(202) 833-5900 • fax: (202) 833-0075
e-mail: information@globalhealth.org
website: www.globalhealth.org

The Global Health Council is a nonprofit membership organization dedicated to improving the health of the two billion people who live on less than $2 a day. The Global Health Council implements programs, delivers health care services, conducts research on key issues, advocates for improved policies and financial support, provides funding for global health programming, and develops lifesaving products. The council publishes *Global Health* magazine, policy briefs, and fact sheets.

International Monetary Fund (IMF)

700 Nineteenth Street NW, Washington, DC   20431
(202) 623-7000 • fax: (202) 623-4661

e-mail: publicaffairs@imf.org
website: www.imf.org

The International Monetary Fund (IMF) is an organization of 186 countries, working to foster global monetary cooperation, secure financial stability, facilitate international trade, promote high employment and sustainable economic growth, and reduce poverty around the world. The IMF monitors the world's economies, lends to members in economic difficulty, and provides technical assistance. The IMF publishes fact sheets, reports on key issues, the *IMF Annual Report*, and the periodical *Finance & Development*, which publishes articles such as "Healing Health Care Finances."

Organisation for Economic Co-operation and Development (OECD)
2, rue André Pascal, 75775 Paris   Cedex 16
   France
(33) 45 24 82 00 • fax: (33) 45 24 85 00
website: www.oecd.org

The Organisation for Economic Co-operation and Development (OECD) works to improve the economic and social well-being of people around the world. The OECD is a membership organization of thirty-four advanced and emerging countries around the world who work to foster global prosperity. The OECD publishes economic surveys and health policy studies about individual nations and studies comparing nations such as *OECD Health Data 2011: Key Indicators*.

Oxfam International
266 Banbury Road, Suite 20, Oxford   OX2 7DL
   United Kingdom
(44) 1865 339 100 • fax: (44) 1865 339 101
e-mail: enquiries@oxfam.org.uk
website: www.oxfam.org

Oxfam International is a confederation of organizations working to end poverty and injustice. Oxfam delivers lifesaving assistance to people affected by natural disasters or conflict and aims to raise public awareness of the causes of poverty. Oxfam publishes numerous research and analysis, available at its website, such as "Living on a Spike: How Is the 2011 Food Price Crisis Affecting Poor People?"

Society for International Development (SID)

1875 Connecticut Avenue NW, Suite 720
Washington, DC   20009
(202) 884-8590 • fax: (202) 884-8499
website: www.sidw.org

The Society for International Development (SID) is a global network of individuals and institutions concerned with development that is participative, pluralistic, and sustainable. SID works with more than one hundred associations, networks, and institutions involving academia, parliamentarians, students, political leaders, and development experts, both at local and international levels, to strive for a better world. SID gathers and disseminates information on innovative development that is published in papers and reports, including the policy brief "Public-Private Sector Partnerships Working for Reproductive Health."

United Nations (UN)

One United Nations Plaza, New York, NY   10017
(212) 906-5000 • fax: (212) 906-5001
website: www.un.org

The United Nations (UN) is an international organization of 193 member states committed to maintaining international peace and security; developing friendly relations among nations; and promoting social progress, better living standards, and human rights. The United Nations spearheaded the development of the Millennium Development Goals, aimed at encouraging development by improving social and economic conditions in the world's poorest countries. The UN publishes numerous annual human development reports and reports on the achievement of the Millennium Development Goals.

World Health Organization (WHO)
Avenue Appia 20, Geneva 27   1211
  Switzerland
(41) 22 791 21 11 • fax: (41) 22 791 31 11
e-mail: info@who.int
website: www.who.int

The World Health Organization (WHO) is the directing and coordinating authority for health within the United Nations system. WHO is responsible for providing leadership on global health matters; shaping the health research agenda; setting norms and standards; articulating evidence-based policy options; providing technical support to countries; and monitoring and assessing health trends. WHO publishes numerous publications, including the annual *World Health Report*, the annual *World Health Statistics*, the monthly *Bulletin of the World Health Organization*, and the *Weekly Epidemiological Record*.

Bibliography of Books

Anne-Emanuelle   *Textbook of International Health: Glo-*
Birn, Yogan Pillay,   *bal Health in a Dynamic World,* 3rd
and Timothy H.   edition. New York: Oxford University
Holtz   Press, 2009.

Steve Brouwer   *Revolutionary Doctors: How Venezuela
and Cuba Are Changing the World's
Conception of Health Care.* New York:
Monthly Review Press, 2011.

John Connell   *The Global Health Care Chain: From
the Pacific to the World.* New York:
Routledge, 2009.

Stephen M.   *Still Broken: Understanding the U.S.
Davidson   Health Care System.* Stanford, CA:
Stanford Business Books, 2010.

Douglas A.   *AIDS, Culture, and Africa.* Gaines-
Feldman, ed.   ville: University Press of Florida,
2008.

Arthur Garson Jr.   *Health Care Half-Truths: Too Many
and Carolyn L.   Myths, Not Enough Reality.* Lanham,
Engelhard   MD: Rowman & Littlefield Publishers, 2007.

Regina E.   *Who Killed Health Care? America's $2
Herzlinger   Trillion Medical Problem and the
Consumer-Driven Cure.* New York:
McGraw-Hill, 2007.

Diana Pinto   *Health Care Systems in Developing
Masis and Peter   and Transition Countries: The Role of
C. Smith, eds.   Research Evidence.* Northampton,
MA: Edward Elgar, 2009.

Padmini Murthy and Clyde Lanford Smith, eds.

Women's Global Health and Human Rights. Sudbury, MA: Jones and Bartlett Publishers, 2010.

Mark Nichter

Global Health: Why Cultural Perceptions, Social Representations, and Biopolitics Matter. Tucson: University of Arizona Press, 2008.

Himanshu Sekhar Rout, ed.

Health Care Systems: A Global Survey. New Delhi: New Century Publications, 2011.

Merrill Singer and G. Derrick Hodge, eds.

The War Machine and Global Health: A Critical Medical Anthropological Examination of the Human Costs of Armed Conflict and the International Violence Industry. Lanham, MD: AltaMira Press, 2010.

Richard Skolnik

Essentials of Global Health. Sudbury, MA: Jones and Bartlett Publishers, 2008.

Ida Susser

AIDS, Sex, and Culture: Global Politics and Survival in Southern Africa. Malden, MA: Wiley-Blackwell, 2009.

Meredeth Turshen

Women's Health Movements: A Global Force for Change. New York: Palgrave Macmillan, 2007.

Yasuo Uchida and Robin Gauld

Health Care Systems in Europe and Asia. New York: Routledge, 2011.

Barbara C. Wallace, ed.

Toward Equity in Health: A New Global Approach to Health Disparities. New York: Springer, 2008.

Rachel E. Walker, ed.	*Health Issues in Eurasia, Europe, and Russia.* New York: Nova Science Publishers, 2011.
Gijs Walraven	*Health and Poverty: Global Health Problems and Solutions.* Washington, DC: Earthscan, 2011.
Linda M. Whiteford and Laurence G. Branch	*Primary Health Care in Cuba: The Other Revolution.* Lanham, MD: Rowman & Littlefield Publishers, 2008.

Index

Geographic headings and page numbers in **boldface** refer to viewpoints about that country or region.